MW00774483

QUIT YOUR BAND

QUIT YOUR BAND

Musical Notes From the Japanese Underground

IAN F. MARTIN

Awai Books
New York and Tokyo

Printed in the United States of America and in the United Kingdom with environmentally responsible paper, including materials certified by the Forest Stewardship Council® and the Sustainable Forestry Initiative®

Published by Awai Books, an imprint of Awai LLC, New York. 1133 Broadway, Suite 708, New York, NY 10010

Copyright © 2016 Ian F. Martin

Publication rights for exclusive English edition of this book arranged by Awai Books/Awai LLC New York

Cover design by CIVILTOKYO's Yuichiro Ito and Takao Neko

Paperback ISBN: 978-1-937220-05-1
E-Book ISBN: 978-1-937220-06-8

Edited by Sandra Flanagan and the Awai Books team with helpful input from Heather Howe.

An Awai Books Trade Paperback Original /// An Awai Books e-book Original. First edition: November 2016

Portrait of Ian F. Martin © 2016 Matt Schley

CONTENTS

A SHORT NOTE ON ARTIST NAMES

As many of you no doubt know, the traditional way Japanese names are rendered is family name first, given name second. But since this book is in English, I have reversed people's names to express them in the Western fashion. When band names are composed of Japanese words, I've transcribed the Japanese into the Roman alphabet phonetically. Where a word is of English or foreign origin, I've adjusted it to the standard English spelling. In cases when a band uses a different name for overseas consumption, I've used both initially and the foreign version thereafter. Lastly, it is common for Japanese bands to use punctuation creatively in their names, often insisting on inserting full stops, random capitalisation and multiple exclamation marks. Where these creative names appear in the body of the text, I've retained punctuation if it doesn't interfere with the meaning of the sentence. In rare cases of bands being annoying and ridiculous with full stops at the end of names, clean copy has taken precedent.

PROLOGUE

"Yamete yaru! Konna bando, yamete yaru!"

Five teenage girls are shrieking these words with a mixture of fury and joy through the frenzied rusty razor slashes of garage-punk guitars, hacking out the odd chord here and there or simply spazzing out in squalls of noise, all thrown together in the kind of chaotic way that suggests that they don't really know how to write songs.

"I'm gonna quit! I'm gonna quit this band!"

This show is part of a tour to promote a compilation album that I'd recently released, and seven years after starting up my label it is easy to feel jaded. The music scene at this time is still operating glumly under the shadow of police crackdowns against clubs that permit dancing after 1:00am. Of the dozen bands featured on my first release at the end of 2005, only one is still regularly performing. It feels like so many years of watching precious talent fall by the wayside, while mediocrities prosper.

And yet here before me is a band in the full flower of youth, celebrating their own demise with such anarchic energy. In a world where pop is primarily composed of bland platitudes urging you to follow your dreams or insisting that friendship is forever, here is something joyously negative, being yelled by a panda-eyed girl in a nightdress that she'd earlier mutilated with safety pins, and another girl still young enough to know that wearing sunglasses indoors is the coolest thing in the world. Everyone in the band has amazing shoes. Oh, and their mothers are sitting at the side of the room with their heads in their hands in shame.

Who cares if it only lasts a moment and is then gone in a blinding flash or a wisp of smoke? Underground music in Japan is beautiful, often nonsensical, and ferociously creative. As a business it's a complete basket case that would have no right to exist under any normal commercial circumstances, and yet it has its own particular ecosystem, its own society, its own economy of sorts, and its own cycle of life. It's given me some of the most exciting music I've ever heard, and it's been an enormous privilege to have been involved, however tangentially, in that world.

This book is not a guide to Japanese music, nor would that even be possible in so slim a volume. You could write an encyclopaedia on the subject and still people would cry out that such and such a band of crucial importance had been omitted. Rather this is at its core a book guided by my own experiences and as a result, I shan't be ashamed of indulging some of my own biases. I hope, however, that I'm also being fair.

Quit Your Band! will go over some key historical movements in Japanese popular music, from the Beatles-influenced "group sounds" movement of the 1960s, to the twin booms of J-Pop and the indie-originated Shibuya-*kei* scene of the 1990s. We'll look at how mainstream and underground music influenced each other over that period, as well as examine the legacy of that music among young musicians today. In addition, I'll try to discuss the ideas of "indie", "alternative", "underground" and "subculture" in the context of Japanese music, looking closely at the world in which musicians nowadays live – examining the live music environment, the information infrastructure, and the social, economic and legal constraints that affect their activities.

Most of this exists below the media radar even in Japan, with alternative or subcultural ideas only emerging piecemeal into the mainstream. In this sense, the creative environment for the most interesting and exciting Japanese music is often as alien to Japanese people as it is to Westerners. Nevertheless, while Japanese media provides its audience with a context, however distorted, Western fans only get to experience Japanese musicians in small out-of-context bites that make it out of short, money-losing overseas tours, brief appearances at festivals like South By Southwest, or by the rare fortune of viral YouTube popularity.

An international sensation on YouTube, the singer Kyary Pamyu Pamyu taps into a historical thread that echoes back to 1980s punk/new wave, 1990s art-pop, and a millennial technopop revival. These musical influences and their historical roots also shape avant-garde acts like the bubblegum noiseniks Melt Banana, who have become a staple of the European and American live circuits. Not as big abroad as in Japan, Tokyo's idol scene also shares historical roots with the avant-garde and it acts as an intersection for both the underground and mainstream – with visible influences running in both directions.

Despite what often seem like the best efforts of the music industry and media to disguise the fact, Japan produces a broad range of the absolute best music in the world. I cannot hope to cover it all, and my recommendations will naturally be coloured by my experiences and tastes. But hopefully the music I discuss here will not only introduce some wonderful artists that readers may not have previously heard, but also provide a platform for analysis that will illuminate the musical culture in which it is made.

PART 1:

HOW I FOUND MY WAY INTO THE JAPANESE
MUSIC SCENE AND WHAT I DISCOVERED
WHEN I GOT THERE

INTRODUCTION

There's an old Hollywood joke that when you're pitching a movie script, whether it's a sci-fi action adventure on a distant planet or a harrowing drama about drug dependency and urban depravation, you always finish the pitch by saying, "In the end, though, this is a story about love."

This book is about music in Japan, in particular about my experiences in the various indie and underground scenes and subscenes that I've found myself involved with over the past decade or so. It touches on history, on the broad narrative sweep of musical culture that goes from Japan's early exposure to Western pop music to its current, impossibly diverse, domestically dominated pop and rock music industry. It deals with money, hardship, greed, and the frustrations inflicted on musicians by cultural and economic forces that exist far out of their ability to control. It is a book about art, passion, struggle and beauty. In the end though, this is a story about love.

My first experience of live Japanese music was on a date. We saw Ex-Girl, an all-female power trio in space-age silver costumes who looked like aliens, moved like robots and claimed to be frogs. Their music seemed to be a mixture of punk, powerpop and opera, and the audience of the 2,700-capacity Zepp Tokyo (all there to see headliners The Strokes) watched Ex-Girl in a mixture of awe and horror. But mostly silence. They went offstage and there was barely a smattering of applause. Seven years later, the date I'd seen the show with was my wife; sometimes the impact of a performance can take a while to pay off.

For all their extraterrestrial wonder, however, Ex-Girl always seemed like too much of an oddity to give me a meaningful "in" into the Japanese indie scene. My appetite was whetted and I was eager to find more, but at the time there was precious little information around, and practically nothing in English. *The Japan Times* was the only media outlet that ever touched on the local alternative music scene, thanks largely to the rambling and excitable articles of peerless Simon Bartz, mostly about rough-edged, tuneless, bawling garage rock freaks with names like Jet Boys, 54 Nude Honeys and Das Boot.

In the end though, the only way to find out anything useful was to just pick a band and dive in. Buy their CD at a show, talk to them, get their email address, and stalk them relentlessly until you find something else worth listening to. Many foreigners who come to Tokyo find one band and immediately adopt them. That band then becomes *their* Japanese band, who they promote to all their friends, maybe even try to help out with a couple of gigs back in their home country, and who they go to see again and again in the same half-empty venues.

Seriously, if you're a no-name Japanese indie band and don't have a pet foreigner, get yourself one. They can be annoying, hanging around like a lost puppy and making your friends feel weird, but they'll love you for the rest of their lives.

Why this happens is hard to know. Partly I suspect it's because as a visitor to a foreign culture, especially one as keen to bombard you day-in-day-out with intangible, superficial, and often alienating cultural information as Japan is, you have a powerful unconscious need for a hook into an aspect of culture that feels grounded, and there's nothing more grounded than a bottom-rung indie band. Every time they try to take flight, they're kicked out of the air and splat back down on the tarmac thanks to a combination of the pressures of working life, the expenses of playing live, and the disinterest of audiences and industry alike. They live on the ground and are rarely even permitted to get off their knees.

And this is perhaps another reason, because a lot of Japanese indie bands are like damaged baby birds, filled with hopeless optimism and naivety, and coloured with an intangible frisson of melancholy and despair. They persevere against impossible odds, creating art and performing it to apathetic audiences that often fail to reach even double figures, burning through insane amounts of money on the venues' impossible ticket quotas, and somehow at the end of it holding onto this kind of hopeless dream that a fairy godmother will float down from the sky and spirit them away into the magical fairyland of record label contract arcadia. You just want to clutch them to your breast and somehow make their dreams reality – they give you the illusion of cultural roots and you give them the illusion of hope.

The band I eventually adopted were called The Students. I'd

first seen them in what I later realised was a freakishly lucky support gig with the always-reliable Shonen Knife. The Students were a sort of new wave trio with the most gloriously off-kilter sense of melody and arrangement, and only the most passing acquaintance with the notion of rehearsal. Their gigs were a tightrope act, with long-term fans constantly keeping a nervous eye on singer Akiko Yoshida's breakable guitar strings. Fans of The Students had to learn a special way of dancing to keep up with the rhythms as they sped up and slowed down in a way that was probably intentional about 37% of the time.

The Students' songs were glorious though. Akiko's vocals had an extraordinary raw quality that always sounded just a little out of key, before the melody resolved itself in such a way as to reveal that no, actually she was singing precisely what she had intended all along. Atsushi Oba's arrangements and snakelike bass solos were genius of a sort that only someone who hasn't got a clue how these things are supposed to be done can pull off, and every moment they were playing, you were immersed in an unstable and frequently catastrophic maelstrom of subtly wrong pop tunes buffeted by ideas straight out of leftfield.

Most importantly, though, stalking The Students gave me my first experience of the real entry-level live music scene of Tokyo. In particular, the venues Rips in the town of Hachioji, out on the remote western fringes of Tokyo, and the slightly more central Koenji Showboat. Koenji in particular was an intoxicating place. Not just the venue, but the whole town was a paradise – narrow pedestrianised streets stacked with bars and boozy *izakayas*, *yakitori* restaurants spilling out onto sidewalks and filling the air with the scent of burned dead bird. I'd never experienced anywhere like it and yet it felt like home the moment I first stepped off the train.

Koenji is also in equal parts famous and notorious as one of the centres of underground music in Japan, host to dozens of venues and music bars, and home to musicians and freaks of all stripes. Through these gigs, I started to find other bands that caught my imagination. There was an unhinged, Pixies-influenced trio called The Glam and a new wave-influenced prog-pop band called Mosquito whose music completely blew apart my ability to define and classify.

Talking to these bands and other gig regulars, I started to notice the names of certain bands recurring, and the one that kept coming up again and again at this time was Number Girl.

THE GENERATION OF 97

The cornerstone of any understanding of what Japanese alternative rock is about today must include the history of three bands: Number Girl, Quruli and Supercar. In 2001-2002 when I first came to Japan, these bands were inescapable, and the cosy live venues of Tokyo were littered with their followers and imitators.

Quruli were the most popular, and the only one of the three still performing at present. Hailing from Kyoto, they had started out in the mid-late 90s as an alt-rock band with a punk edge, releasing a couple of albums on indie labels before signing to major label Victor Entertainment's Speedstar imprint. Their first album for Victor, *Sayonara Stranger*, was a solid enough, if clearly rather cleaned-up and sanitised indie rock record, but the Jim O'Rourke-produced follow-up, 2000's *Zukan*, remains one of the most oft-cited influences for contemporary alt-rock bands. 2001's *Team Rock* and especially 2002's magnificent *The World is Mine* went still further, incorporating more dance and electronic influences, before the band seemed to retreat from such ambition and experimentation. They gradually began to retool themselves as a comforting but rarely-remarkable folk-rock songbook.

Supercar formed at around the same time as Quruli, but in the city of Aomori in northeastern Japan. They made a splash in 1998 with their epic debut album *Three Out Change*, a sprawling mess of shoegaze and warped, distorted pop melodies that just pounds you in the face for 78 minutes and then cuts suddenly short in the middle of an extended guitar wig-out. As with Quruli, Supercar explored a more electronic direction over subsequent albums, with the more restrained *Jump Up* following in 1999 and another gloriously overblown mess of an album, *Futurama*, following in 2000. 2002's *Highvision* was a honing of *Futurama*'s confusion of disco, new wave and indie rock ideas into something a bit more coherent (and less interesting), while 2004's *Answer* played like an extended funeral march for a band too tired to press on but possessed of too restless an imagination to go quietly. Supercar's music always existed in the hypnogogic realm between sleep and wake, and this influence can be seen in any number of dreamy indie-dance acts, particularly musicians on the fringes of the anime music world who were evidently attracted by the washed-out, dreamy textures of Supercar music and lyrics. These fans refused to take *Answer* as a cue to wake up and to move on, preferring instead to retreat from the tension of that dawn borderland and take the group's demise as merely the first movement in an eternal dream.

Number Girl were probably the least commercially successful of the three bands, but in the alternative scene of the early 2000s their influence was everywhere. Led by charismatic anti-frontman Shutoku Mukai, Number Girl hailed from Fukuoka, the opposite end of the country from Supercar. There was a lively punk and alternative scene already in Fukuoka, with bands like Panicsmile, Mo'some Tonebender and Rumtag all active at about that time, and the teenage Ringo Shiina a regular fixture in the audiences of gigs at the scene hotspot of Vivre Hall, where many local musicians both played and worked as staff. Mukai's lyrics were abstract, disaffected sketches of youth, violence and boredom, and they touched a nerve with the generation coming of age around the turn of the millennium. Hisako Tabuchi's wilfully discordant guitars and Mukai's tormented, out-of-tune vocals were the opposite of everything 90s J-Pop stood for, and their overt cheerleading for US alternative artists like Hüsker Dü, Pixies and Iggy Pop marked them as the homegrown answer to the likes of Sonic Youth and Nirvana that many kids were crying out for.

By the time of Number Girl's final album, 2002's *Num Heavymetallic*, the band were experimenting with more funk-influenced rhythms, reminiscent of UK postpunkers like The Pop Group, and when the band broke up the following year, the four members all took quite different paths. Tabuchi joined Bloodthirsty Butchers, a band which had been a big influence on early Number Girl, later forming the poppier Toddle and joining with members of Supercar to form Lama. Number Girl Bassist Kentaro Nakao played with numerous bands including the wonderfully named Sloth Love Chunks, and the hard rock- and metal-influenced post-hardcore band Crypt City. Nakao also went onto became a regular collaborator with garage-punk queen Aiha Higurashi (Loves, The Girl, Seagull Screaming Kiss Her Kiss Her). Drummer Ahito Inazawa formed the new wave-influenced Vola and the Oriental Machine. These successor bands, especially those who stayed on indie labels, found themselves welcomed back into the scene as elder statesmen of a sort, and it became not uncommon to find a group like Toddle or Crypt City playing with smaller bands at venues like Club Goodman, Fever or Three. As much as the likes of Tabuchi or Nakao might want to be judged purely on the music they are now making, their previous band's work and influence casts a long shadow and there is still an undoubted thrill a young band and their fans might get from finding their heroes so accessible.

Mukai of Number Girl went on to experiment in new ways of making music, founding his own "Matsuri Studio" and recruiting old Fukuoka mates Panicsmile as a backing band for a series of solo shows. He also played with instrumental funk-alternative band 54-71 in the first lineup of his new band Zazen Boys (whose existence in this form actually overlaps slightly with the end of Number Girl). Zazen Boys eventually coalesced into a new band entirely, with Inazawa coming back on drums for the first couple of albums. Zazen Boys were more popular than Number Girl ever were, but somehow they meant less. For whatever reason, Zazen Boys were first and foremost about the music – and they were amazing musicians, their songs intelligently constructed, overwhelming you with the skill and virtuosity on display without really compromising the essentially discordant quality of Mukai's voice. Still, it felt as if Mukai no longer wanted to be the voice of a generation, that he had decided to develop his artistic voice within the more abstract confines of the music industry rather than within the tumultuous hearts of Japan's confused millennials.

So my arrival in Japan coincided almost exactly with the cresting of the wave led by what I'm choosing to call the "Generation of 97". The music scene I discovered in its wake was composed to a great degree of its frothing backwash. Some bands sanded down the edges and made cleaner, more streamlined, major-friendly pop out of its influence, while others pushed it further, into more imaginative or discordant extremes, but it seemed at the time as if everybody was touched by it somehow. Quruli, Supercar and Number Girl had shown that Japanese rock bands could take on the British and American alternative bands of the 90s at their own game and come out of it with their heads held high, and in doing so, they had laid new ground for Japanese rock to develop in its own way from this point on.

WRITING ABOUT JAPANESE MUSIC

In the early 2000s, I was fairly regularly checking out the Tokyo dates of hip UK and US bands who were visiting Japan on tour, in addition to following a handful of local bands around a series of cramped basements. Slowly, I came to terms with those major label bands like Supercar and Number Girl that hung suspended somewhere between mainstream acceptance and the indie scene. It was in this environment that I first started writing about music.

It was a hobby at first: just an attempt to document some of the music I was listening to and impose some sort of order on my thoughts about it. From the start, I felt it was important to write about Japanese music not as a weak imitation, nor as something alien and unknowable, but as artists in the same basic world and on equal terms with overseas bands.

Noble though these intentions were, I soon realised that the same set of references and terminology I used to talk about British music, imported from my teenage years reading the *NME* (a then-influential British music paper), were insufficient tools to write about what many bands in Japan were doing. In the absence of any pre-existing body of reference material, I started inventing new terms to describe what I was hearing around me.

Looking at these embarrassing early efforts now, they're littered with attempts to define Japanese bands in terms of references to contemporary UK or US rock music that they had no relevant connection with, or using genre-terms I'd half-jokingly coined for my own convenience. I was once cornered by someone who had been reading over my old blog entries and was fascinated by the term "enka-punk", wondering if there was a whole new genre he'd never discovered. Nope, it's just the first thing that popped into my head when I was trying to describe music influenced by the singer Ringo Shiina that combined melodies reminiscent of older Japanese pop with rock or garage style guitars and rhythms – the kind of music that you could find all over the place in the mid-2000s, but which didn't (and still doesn't) have a satisfactory name.

In fact it wasn't only my weak sense of context for Japanese music that troubled me but my lack of any real understanding of American music. Coming of age in the UK during mid-90s Britpop meant that American music was strictly off limits, so there was a whole world of music that I just hadn't really experienced until Graham from Blur told me it was OK to like Pavement. American music was a huge influence on the Japanese rock scene though, and I had to play a swift game of catch-up to process it all. While I sometimes use the terms interchangeably, this divide between British and US music in the 90s is probably at the heart of the slightly different inflections the words "indie" and "alternative" have for me. The former is a word I associate with the *NME*, and it suggests to me something not necessarily gentler, but perhaps more melodic, more British. The latter is a word I associate with MTV, and it calls to mind some heavier, dirtier, more American. It was only after spending time in Japan that the word "underground" took on particular meaning, partly due to the literally subterranean nature of so many venues, but mostly due to the way interesting and exciting sounds are generally kept with such fastidious efficiency from contact with the mainstream.

The sense of the underground as something isolated extended beyond the mainstream/non-mainstream dichotomy and into the whole landscape and history of music in Japan – it all felt so compartmentalised and disconnected. One thing that continued to bug me was the way the musicians and other fans around me, while certainly not ignorant of the music of the past, didn't seem to have any real sense of the story of Japanese music.

Any music fan growing up in Britain in the 90s would have had a fairly solid general sense of British music's development, starting with the importation of American rock'n'roll, the explosion of bands that came with The Beatles, the development of psychedelia into progressive rock, the appearance of glam, then punk's reaction against the excesses of the 70s, the development of punk into new wave, the birth of indie rock, acid house, and then all of these coming together in Manchester. That story may have been very simplified, but it left you with a more or less useful framework with which to understand most UK rock of the 90s, and which with embellishments and extra research could be augmented to understand a lot of other music as well. TV shows like *Rock Family Trees* plotted the interrelationships of certain scenes and bands, while chart show

Top of the Pops ran a weekly supplementary show of archive performances, and music magazines bombarded you with top 100 lists of the most important or influential albums or artists of all time on what sometimes seemed like a weekly basis. Though the results were often inaccurate and coloured by nostalgia, British music culture placed a great deal of importance on its past, and in doing so, imbued music fans with a sense of narrative into which music could be contextualised.

In comparison to Britain, the music press in Japan has no real culture of criticism. One of the formative memories I have of music journalism is a review in *NME* from the late 90s of the album *Cobra and Phases Group Play Voltage in the Milky Night* by Anglo-French Marxist indie aesthetes Stereolab, who remain to this day one of my favourite bands of all time. The review began with the line, "You have to admit they're good at what they do. But then so was Hitler." The write-up ended with the score "0/10".

There was something thrilling about the bald, crude, hyperbolic audacity of that opening line and the cold, clinical numerical coda. To this day, I know never to take seriously anything the writer of that review has to say about music, but thinking back on it still forces me to do a little mental shuffle, justifying to myself what it is that I like about the band. That brutal contrary opinion is at once funny to read, and also helps sharpen my own sense of why I like the music.

In Japan, openly negative reviews are more or less taboo. Number Girl/Crypt City's Kentaro Nakao told me in an interview, "The worst review I ever had was on an info card in

[CD rental store] Tsutaya. It wasn't exactly bad: it just read, 'I have no idea what's going on here.'"

So confused or ironic comments from minimum-wage CD store employees aside, there are basically two kinds of Japanese music reviews. The first type are the little mini-reviews that feature in fashion or general culture magazines. These are basically copied directly from press releases by overworked or lazy writers who have no particular knowledge of or interest in music – check through a few different magazines and you'll see the exact same wording come up again and again. These reviews are essentially worthless. They're little advertisements designed to teach readers the cultural accessories they need to go with their new outfits.

The other type are the sort that appear in music magazines like *Rockin' On Japan*, and these are worth paying a little bit more attention to. On the surface, they're not that different from the reviews in fashion magazines – short, descriptive reviews that don't analyse the music in any critical way – but they also provide insight into the way rock music business in Japan operates.

When it started out in the 1970s, *Rockin' On* was a genuinely revolutionary magazine. It covered new Western rock bands like King Crimson and Led Zeppelin, which people simply couldn't get detailed information about from more mainstream sources. *Rockin' On* also carried important debates about the internal politics of music and the direction it should take. Even in the 1970s, however, compromises were being made in the music press, and the idea that labels could pay to feature their bands took hold pretty early in the industry's history. As the 1970s wore

31

on, sponsorship money and industry power increasingly compromised the newly formed music press' neutrality, with only the fiercely independent *Rock Magazine* really standing out from its more industry-influenced rivals. In 1986, *Rockin' On* split off its foreign and Japanese music coverage into separate publications, and the sister magazine *Rockin' On Japan* came about. This domestically-focused version of the magazine, along with two annual musical events it hosts — the *Rock in Japan Festival* every August and the *Count Down Japan* festival every December – makes *Rockin' On Japan* a leading forum through which new Japanese rock can get noticed. This position, particularly after the closure of many rival music magazines in the 2000s, means that Japanese labels have little choice but to suck up to *Rockin' On Japan* in return for coverage in their magazine and consideration for its festival lineups. At the same time, magazines like *Rockin' On* are left entirely dependent on industry money to maintain their business model.

That's not to say that good journalism doesn't sometimes happen in Japan, but there are obvious conflicts of interest within the music media. Journalists are unable to write honestly about music and readers subsequently can't believe a word they read. Meanwhile, many labels hate the magazines and can't wait for the system of payment for coverage to crash and burn. For artists themselves, the problem is subtler. Buoyed by false praise, they are deprived of any of the creative tension between critic and artist that might otherwise help keep them on their toes. Despite often coming across as obnoxious clowns, critics can perform a useful role in forcing listeners and artists to ask questions of themselves while helping to prevent the creative process from stagnating and descending into a dreary retread of tired old tropes. But when critics work as mouthpieces for the music industry, tropes become codified at all levels and music becomes homogenised and watered down as a result.

Still, simply criticising the current system doesn't necessarily mean a workable alternative would be easy to come by, and there are some other issues to consider.

Firstly, the business model whereby labels pay magazines for coverage was not something built up purely out of greed. It's a rare magazine that can sustain itself on advertising and sales alone, and when you pay for a feature, you're essentially paying the writer's salary – *Rock Magazine* in the 70s and 80s was run almost entirely by volunteers. One alternative nowadays might be to look to the web – in particular the model pioneered by *Pitchfork* in the US. New sites like the indie-focused *ki-ft* and *IndieGrab* might be able to fill this role, although there are good reasons to be sceptical. *Pitchfork* built its reputation and identity at a particular time in the web's development, and it's debatable whether a new site would be able to replicate that success now. Instead, what usually seems to happen is that a site begins with good intentions of covering undiscovered and underground music, but once the picture painted by the diagnostics stats begins to become clearer, they find themselves chasing page views into the predictable fields of idol music, middle-of-the-road indie pop/rock or whatever is already popular. With the bulk of traffic coming from short news items, usually derived closely from press releases, music sites' influence is often limited to simply curating information – not a useless role, but not an agenda-driving one either. The Japanese language site *Natalie* seems to have made a success of drawing in page views through coverage of online buzz-friendly genres, and as a result seems to have found a sustainable business model. However, it clearly faces a constant tension between the instant and visible feedback its pages draw and the risks it knows it must take to be on the crest of the next wave. As a result, even such a popular and high visibility site has limited power to drive the agenda.

A media outlet that already has a reputation off which to trade might be able to carry more weight. The web magazine *Cookie Scene* is one outlet that could have formed the basis of a more powerful and influential online indie music hub if it had been developed further. Starting out as a print magazine, it retreated onto the web over the course of 2009-2010 but continued to post long, in-depth, analytical music reviews that offer a refreshing alternative to the reheated press releases that account for pretty much all other music writing in Japan. While the online version adopted a non-profit operational model and focused more on overseas artists, an expanded *Cookie Scene* could have provide an upscale, music-focused complement to more news-based, less critically-minded and curatorial sites like *Natalie* and *Ototoy*, and the more generalised pop culture and subculture coverage of *Cinra*.

Another important issue to consider is that even if some sort of financially viable music press that didn't rely on content paid for by labels were to emerge, it would be foolish to think for even a moment that the record companies would give up the control they exert over what journalists write. The industry standard of requiring journalists to submit articles to the label for "checking" is deeply embedded in both record company and journalistic practice, and major labels and talent agencies regularly use their control over the publication rights of artist photos and album jackets to ensure that the content of articles is acceptable to them.

Indeed, control over image rights and information for a long time even extended to the artists themselves. In an interview, Aiha Higurashi of Seagull Screaming Kiss Her Kiss Her told me of her first-hand experiences during her time with Sony in the early-to-mid 2000s.

"Each photo, they had the license of my image," Higurashi explains, "so even if I wanted to use one photo, I had to ask them to upload it. Myspace was a big thing then, but I couldn't do Myspace or any social networking."

If that was the sort of control labels extended over their own artists, one can imagine the degree of micromanaging they are accustomed to exerting over the media. This control of images also allows labels and talent agencies to strategically use permissions for their bigger artists as a lever to negotiate favourable coverage of their less established acts.

The only way I can see the media being able to cultivate a more critical music culture is if a magazine, or more likely a web site, were able to reach a position of influence independently of music industry interference. If there were a self-sufficient magazine that fostered a carefully considered, non-sensationalist critical culture among its writers, Japanese readers would likely

35

accept a more honest and confrontational style. I'm suspicious of the cliché that Japanese culture values harmony above all else. While there is some truth to this platitude in the world of popular music, this truth doesn't reflect an immutable Japanese tradition but rather than the more mundane machinations of consumer capitalism.

Japanese arts and literature have a vibrant and frequently harsh critical culture, and it is only in the carefully managed business environments of pop culture where critical analysis is seen as taboo. Pop music as practiced by major labels and talent agencies, and as presented on TV variety shows, is marketed as pure entertainment. Behind the scenes, these companies micromanage the media narratives and ensure coverage is suitably fluffy and inconsequential, and as a result, audience expectations have adjusted themselves to the world inside the bubble that the industry has created around itself and its products.

One precondition of building a healthier critical culture around music would have to be normalising the idea that popular music can be art, therefore opening it up to the same kind of critical tools that Japanese culture is happy to accept in other fields.

Some people would no doubt complain that this is simply a case of elitists imposing their own interpretation of pop culture on fans who just want to be entertained – a sort of *"Wah! Mummy, the bad man is trying to make me think!"* response – but in an ideal world, both kinds of reporting would be able to exist side by side. Just as there are many kinds of music, there ought to be many different ways of looking at music.

With the music press driven by the commercial needs of labels to constantly push fresh product, and with editors' reluctance to be seen as giving favour to one label or artist over others, the idea of critically assessing the value of music in a historical or genre context has tended to feel alien to the scene's journalistic culture.

One crack in this monochromatic way of doing things occurred in 2007, when Daisuke Kawasaki of *Rolling Stone Japan* published the first ever list of the Top 100 Japanese Albums of All Time. The article broke a code of silence, an omertà that had previously prevented the ranking of music in Japan.

The list was informed by some of its author's own biases, and Japanese music fans could find lots to quibble with. However, while there were some questionable choices and omissions, the main purpose of the list was not to be definitive. Rather, the list sought to start a discussion that might eventually lead towards some kind of historical canon of Japanese rock. *Snoozer* magazine followed up grudgingly with its own list of 150 albums, and between the two lists, a cohesive picture started to emerge of certain bands, artists and musical movements. Most importantly, the rankings also served as platforms for debate about the history of Japanese rock music.

So where does Japanese rock actually start?

PART 2:

A COMPREHENSIVE AND COMPLETELY ACCURATE ACCOUNT OF THE ENTIRE HISTORY OF POPULAR MUSIC IN JAPAN

EARLY DEVELOPMENTS IN JAPANESE POPULAR MUSIC

Before the Second World War, there was a form of popular music known as *ryūkōka*, which sought to combine Japanese folk melodies and Western popular music, with the influence of jazz beginning to creep in as Japan moved into the 1930s. However, it is in the postwar era that the foundations of popular music as we now know it were laid.

The two most important structural influences on the development of pop music in post-war Japan were the US military and the yakuza.

From 1945 to 1952, Japan was under occupation by the United States, which subsequently retained a strong military presence in the country. Military bases became entry points for American pop culture, particularly jazz, and music venues appeared in order to entertain soldiers around the country.

The people who controlled access for artists to these venues were the yakuza. The relationship between the US military, the yakuza and the entertainment industry at this time is a murky one to say the least, but it can at least be said that the yakuza took advantage of the postwar situation to carve themselves a secure position as middlemen between performers and infrastructure. Kazuo Taoka of the Yamaguchi-gumi was, in addition to being godfather of the most powerful crime syndicate in the country, a powerful impresario who guided the career of the young singer Hibari Misora.

Hibari Misora holds a pretty much eternally unshakeable position as the greatest and most beloved pop singer in Japanese music history, and her music defined the sound of postwar Japanese popular music. Jazz strengthened its hold on Japanese popular music, and the term *kayōkyoku* became the established genre for the new, more Western-oriented singers of the day. The more traditional-sounding, weepy balladeering type of popular song began to gradually shuffle off into its own category, which would eventually become established as *enka*. Both *kayōkyoku* and *enka* were still the heavily produced and carefully managed products of a nascent industry, but as they started to come into their own, more rebellious musical styles were infiltrating Japan from overseas.

ROCK'N'ROLL ARRIVES IN JAPAN

As rock'n'roll exploded in America and Britain, its fruits began to make their way into the Japanese music world. Rockabilly experienced a short-lived boom in the late 1950s before being stamped out by the authorities, but elements of it nevertheless found their way into the mainstream via singers like Kyu Sakamoto, thus setting in motion the cycle of repression followed by sanitisation and co-option that would become standard practice over the decades to come.

After rockabilly, the next big wave from the West was the surfy instrumental guitar music of bands like The Shadows and The Ventures (the latter of whom have been able to use Japan as a cash cow for decades). Known in Japanese as *eleki*, an abbreviation of "electric guitar music", surfy instrumental riffs from Britain and America inspired a generation of Japanese musicians. The master of the *eleki* craft was Takeshi Terauchi, who took the form beyond many of his Western counterparts, pushing surf at times into the realms of classical, folk music and psychedelia.

The arrival of The Beatles in 1966 to play Tokyo's prestigious Budokan martial arts venue prompted another upheaval, and suddenly instrumental guitars and reverb were out and floppy fringes were in. The music that sprang up in the wake of The Beatles was known as "group sounds" or GS and it comprises what we might call the final stage of Japanese rock and pop's prehistory.

Group sounds was still heavily rooted in the influence of foreign music, in this case British beat music of the 1960s, but many of the musicians involved would form the core of the subsequent generation and play a role in forging a distinctive Japanese musical identity. The most popular GS performers were probably The Tigers, although from a critical perspective they are notable primarily for their willingness to do whatever record companies asked as long as it made them famous. Starting out as a more or less Beatles-influenced rock'n'roll band, they were quickly assimilated into the prevailing *kayōkyoku* mainstream with singer Kenji "Julie" Sawada going on to have a successful solo career.

The Tigers' main rivals in the world of GS were The Tempters, although The Spiders probably have a more enduring legacy. The Mops were another key band of the era, but the group sounds band that stands out best in retrospect was probably The Golden Cups, whose brutal, fuzz-drenched garage rock was way too freaky for the music industry of the time, the core of which was still built around touring nice, well-dressed jazz singers and their backing bands through the US military base circuit. The Golden Cups' version of much covered punk-garage classic "Hey Joe" is sensational, with its proto-Sonic Youth guitar noise squalls and absolutely psychotic bass playing.

Group sounds retains a small but notable influence in the Japanese indie world, forming a subset of the garage/mod scene, a retro music and fashion subculture that painstakingly recreates the sounds of the 1960s. The influence of group sounds has also crept into the fringes of the mainstream over the past few years with The Captains exploiting its image by dressing up in red Sgt. Pepper-esque uniforms and Kinoko Hotel donning mini-skirted versions of basically the same thing, although tellingly, neither band makes exclusively group sounds-influenced music.

In fact, it seems that the affection many have for group sounds lies more in the idea of what it was than its musical legacy. The music itself was too derivative at one end of the spectrum and too easily subsumed by *kayōkyoku* and what gets more generally called *Shōwa pops* at the other. For example, as great as The Golden Cups were, they still relied heavily on mimicking and covering Anglo-American rock'n'roll. Meanwhile, the aforementioned group sounds performers Tigers and Kenji Sawada never really succeeeded in musically distinguishing themselves from *kayōkyoku*.

In terms of image, the inclusion of foreign and mixed race members in group sounds bands served as a badge of authenticity. This preference towards a foreign racial aesthetic, on stage and on album jackets, illustrates the extent to which the genre was conscious of its alien origins and sought to exploit that exotic appeal.

It's interesting to note that despite the importance of group sounds in domesticating rock'n'roll in Japan, both the previously mentioned *Rolling Stone Japan* and *Snoozer* lists give short shrift to it in terms of the music. What the lists lauded were those new rock bands from the late 1960s onwards that helped move Japanese rock on from straight imitation into something that was beginning to develop on its own terms.

NEW ROCK

While group sounds bands tried to play up their foreign credentials, often with vocalists of Western ancestry, bands from the 1970s onwards increasingly began to sing in Japanese and the language itself had an impact on the sound of their music. An important band in this next stage of Japanese rock's evolution is The Jacks – perhaps the first great Japanese rock band. The song *Marianne*, off their classic debut album, usually known in Japan as *Jacks no Sekai* and in the West as *Vacant World*, is a masterpiece, with the rhythm section and guitars slipping loosely in and out of tempo. The result is both unnerving, exciting, and deeply, heavily psychedelic.

The Jacks were also defiantly anti-mainstream, prone to wearing sunglasses at scandalously impractical times of day, and generally as far away from the sort of thing the talent agency system knew how to deal with as was possible in 1968. It should come as no surprise that no one in Japan could have given a monkey's arse about The Jacks in their heyday except for arty, beret-wearing poetry students, all of whom went on to form bands.

One of these bands was the legendary and legendarily mysterious Les Rallizes Dénudés (known as *Hadaka no Rallizes* in Japan).

The 1970s were when Japanese music, both pop and rock, really came into its own creatively. The Jacks were important pioneers, but their brand of brooding, nonconformist psychedelia was taken way further by Les Rallizes Dénudés. Rallizes are regarded by a lot of people in the contemporary underground and alternative scene as fathers of Japanese noise rock and even as a sort of proto-shoegaze. Their music was raw, scrappy and brutal, not so much drenched in feedback as aflame with it, and like The Jacks, they looked dangerously, transgressively cool.

They were also associated with some pretty intense politics, specifically the *Nihon Sekigun* or Japanese Red Army, and in one particularly notorious incident one of their numerous bass players, Moriaki Wakabayashi, was part of a gang who hijacked a Boeing 727 passenger aircraft at Fukuoka airport and flew it to North Korea. As with the Baader Meinhof Gang associations that dogged elements of the contemporary German *kosmische* scene, bands like Rallizes Dénudés and the similarly political Zuno Keisatsu were forced to operate under near constant police surveillance and a social environment that continued to see them as potentially dangerous terrorists.

There were a lot of heavy bands from this period that can be loosely classified together under the label new rock. Notable artists include Flower Travellin' Band, Speed, Glue & Shinki, Murahachibu, and theatrical composer J.A.Seazer[*].

The intersection between underground theatre and rock in the 1970s is of crucial importance, with the intellectually questioning sensibility of the former playing a key role in prodding and provoking the development of the latter. One artist who came of age in the 1970s was the musician and actor Koichi Makigami, who first toured the US and UK with the theatrical troupe Tokyo Kid Brothers before returning to Tokyo to begin his own legendary musical career with the band Hikashu.

Speaking to Makigami for this book, he explained that, "Shuji Terayama made a sort of rock musical, *Throw Away Your Books, Rally in the Streets*, and the soundtrack was really good. It had Western things and Japanese things mixed, which was a big influence. Terayama worked with Yuya Uchida, members of Flower Travellin' Band, J.A.Seazer, Kan Mikami, and these people were all asking, 'What is Japanese rock?'"

Musicians had different answers to this question and Yuya Uchida's ideas about Japanese rock would prove formative.

As a producer of somewhat respectable but nevertheless underground music, Uchida was at the heart of one of the key debates around the birth of Japanese rock: the question of language. In the early 1970s, the newly established music press carried arguments about the appropriate language of rock music with Uchida arguing that English was rock's mother tongue and

---

[*] Many of these artists were discussed entertainingly, if rather fancifully, by Julian Cope in his excellent book *Japrocksampler*.

that real rock needed to be sung in English, while a young musician called Haruomi Hosono from the folk-rock band Happy End argued that Japanese musicians needed to find a way of making rock work in their native tongue.

Given the dominance of Japanese language music in the country now, it would be easy to say that Hosono's argument won, although no public debate of this sort was ever decided simply by one side having the better argument, and in the end I suspect it was commercial pressures that decided the result in his favour.

Outside of the commercial arena, however, the question of language remains, and whenever new musical styles are imported from abroad, an evolutionary fork opens up between those who cleave to its foreign roots and those who seek to naturalise it. Part of this is because those musicians most in touch with overseas music are by nature more likely to speak English in the first place. It's rare that a foreign band publishes information about themselves in Japanese, so first-adopters from Japan all need some English ability. These first-adopters tend to feel comfortable singing in English and they are likely to consider English to be more authentic than Japanese, since they have early exposure to musical root sources.

As a musical style becomes more popular and native traditions begin to form and become codified, new musicians find themselves with a much greater pool of local influences to draw on and far less need to search overseas for new material, so singing in Japanese comes to feel like a more natural thing to do. This, of course, then feeds the appeal of the foreign version of the music again, as the co-option by the dominant Japanese mainstream strips the music of its alternative appeal.

So in the 70s, Western influences were still strong, but rock music in Japan was working its way towards its own identity. This is also where we start to see agreement forming among critics over the important early works in the Japanese rock canon, with The Jacks and "new rock" bands like Murahachibu and Flower Travellin' Band making both the *Rolling Stone Japan* and *Snoozer* "best of all time" lists, and Snoozer also including Les Rallizes Dénudés and Zuno Keisatsu. Tellingly, The Jacks' debut is the *only* 1960s album featured in either list.

ROCK'N'ROLL AND THE SMELL OF GASOLINE

One thing the "new rock" bands had in common was that they tended to be very serious. They eschewed the simple pop thrills that had characterised the group sounds generation in favour of heavy riffs, heavy politics, or some combination of both. The 1970s was a time when rock and pop were as far apart, as defiantly opposed, as they could be. Some bands held on to rock'n'roll's fun-loving spirit though, and in the process pointed new routes into both the mainstream and the future of the underground.

Petroleum-fuelled riff merchants Rouge were like a Japanese New York Dolls. And Gedou were the living embodiment of every biker's fantasies. Far from the comfortable dadrocker he is now, Eikichi Yazawa of Carol came over as a generation-defining rebel and every father's nightmare of the kind of monster her daughter might one day bring home. In fact, more than any other artists of the 1970s, Yazawa and Carol spanned the divide between the unacceptable underground and marketable mass culture, to achieve status as icons of their generation. There may have been something a bit prefab about the rebellion peddled by Yazawa and Carol, but it placed a wedge into the doorway of the

Japanese entertainment world that would allow a trickle of ideas to find their way from the underground into TV studios and major label recording studios for the next musical generation.

Artists like RC Succession, who gained traction in the 1970s from a more folk-influenced starting point, would occupy a similar position on the pivot between mainstream acceptance and dangerous rebellion. Until his death in 2009, RC Succession singer Kiyoshiro Imawano continued to embody contrarian ideas, unlike many others of his generation who became more thoroughly subsumed by the mainstream.

Outside of the music money machine in Tokyo, other cities offered alternate visions of rock modernity. In early 1970s Fukuoka, there was a generation of musicians coming of age with little interest in what was going on in the nation's capital, preferring a cocktail of obscure Mississippi blues imports and new rock direct from Britain and America.

Formed in 1970, the Fukuoka band Sonhouse were one of the first of what became known as "*mentai* rock" (after Fukuoka's local spicy fish egg delicacy). Makoto Ayukawa, guitarist and founding member of Sonhouse as well as the legendary later band Sheena & The Rokkets, has claimed that the sense of freedom 1970 American documentary *Woodstock* was a catalyst for change. The sense of freedom that the film encapsulated, and the feeling that culture is something you can go out and create yourself, are powerful ideas with significance beyond the hippy movement.

While the 1970s rock'n'rollers of the *mentai* rock scene were still very much copying Western music, what was starting happening here was kids deciding, "Hey, anyone can be in a band and anyone can play music... ME TOO!" and this, for want of a better word, is punk.

FROM A DRUG BUST TO NEW MUSIC

But let's not get ahead of ourselves. Many 1970s rockers are revered among musical journalists today, but their bands had meant squat in mainstream Japanese culture. Other artists took a more commercial direction, and the forking off of the 1970s Japanese music scene into underground and mainstream was exemplified by the fate of one famous rock musical.

The musical *Hair* had, during its brief run in Japan, sent the Japanese establishment into a state of apoplectic terror. *Hair* was seen as a step towards the inevitable transformation of the nation's youth into feral, priapic half-beasts who feed by injecting LSD into their eyeballs. However, it had also been a forum where many talented musicians were drawn together, thanks in no small part to the efforts of the musical's producer, hippy scenester Shōrō Kawazoe.

Naturally, given the high concentration of hippy weirdniks involved, the police were keen to stop *Hair*, and an early drug raid that turned up small quantities of marijuana gave them the excuse they needed to shut down the show after only a few performances. Many musicians were understandably pissed off that their meal ticket had been snatched away, with some turning to the "new rock" scene, while others took a more commercial turn and went pro.

The gradual recruitment of these originally hippy-influenced musicians, as well as others of their generation, into the pool of songwriters and session musicians that talent agencies would use came to define the sound of mainstream pop in the 1970s. Parallel to the mainstreaming of the hippies was the growth of folk singer-songwriters performing in a style known as *yojohan* (named after the four and a half tatami mat sized rooms that were typical lodging spaces for young musicians). The result of the industry's gradual cooption of these underground styles was a gradual emergence of a pop genre that the always imaginative press dubbed "new music". Artists that exemplify it include Folk Crusaders, Takuro Yoshida, Yosui Inoue, Miyuki Nakajima, Amii Ozaki, the transcendental Yumi Arai and others.

The band, however, that probably did more than any other to establish the building blocks of new Japanese pop and rock music in the early 1970s is Happy End. They pioneered a mode of songwriting that took the strictly syllabic nature of Japanese language lyrics and combined it with Western-influenced folk rock melodies in a one-syllable-one-note rhythmical form. Happy End were revolutionary, and echoes of their sound can now be felt everywhere nowadays, from the folk-tinged rock and indie of artists like Quruli, Kenta Maeno and Shugo Tokumaru to the songwriting clichés that mainstream artists nowadays regularly bore us with.

The Japanisation of rock was further developed in the late 1970s by the band Southern All Stars, who wedded their

Japanese lyrics to an affected, Anglicised pronunciation style. For many, this stylised pronunciation provided an answer to the old problem of how to make rock music work in Japanese. Even if the present day appeal of much "new music" is essentially nostalgic – and there is some dismal, sentimental rubbish – it also left Japanese pop with a canon of classic artists and played an important role in developing a musical vocabulary for Japanese pop and rock music that endures to this day.

POP COMES OF AGE AND ENKA OSSIFIES

As underground songwriters percolated into the mainstream and scored some hits in the 1970s, Japanese pop – known as *kayōkyoku* – was entering a golden age. *Kayōkyoku* had grown distinct as something modern and Western-influenced, and it contrasted with other mainstream musical genres like *enka*, which by this point referred to melodramatic ballads that carried a more Japanese and traditional image. Artists would still dabble with both styles, but it was usually pretty easy to tell which way a record would go by looking at its cover photo (kimono meant *enka*, while fashionable, modern clothes meant *kayōkyoku*), and as the 1970s wore on, *enka* became a discrete thing cut off from and increasingly irrelevant to modern pop.

The Japanese media will, even today, occasionally run spurious stories about how "young people are getting into *enka* again" and if you encounter stories like this, you should dismiss them for what they are: desperate, lying rubbish. The problem with *enka* is that it's just far too inflexible. It's often inaccurately described as "Japanese country & western" but while anyone with a guitar and a sad story can become a country singer, to do *enka* properly you need a full orchestra. When the black

56

American singer Jero debuted as an *enka* vocalist in the 2000s, much was made of him wearing hip hop clothing, but nothing he did musically added anything significant to a genre that's been preserved in aspic for decades. Jero's devotion to the form of *enka* wasn't followed by a modernising wave of hip hop deconstructions. In the end, the American singer was a novelty act to most people and he left the genre much as he found it.

The ossification of *enka* and its branding as "traditional Japanese music" tends nowadays to disguise the foreign origin of many of its foundational pre-1960s influences, but the process of shaking off foreign influences was underway in the poppier world of *kayōkyoku* too. With many of them having roots in the then vibrant new rock and new music scenes, the songwriters behind many *kayōkyoku* hits had moved past imitation and were ready to start making something of their own.

The structure of the pop industry was also about to experience a shakeup due to the technological disruption of TV. Up until the 1970s, the visibility of bands was largely limited to a circuit of venues centred around American military bases. Access to this network had been controlled almost exclusively by one talent agency, Watanabe Productions (colloquially known as "Nabepro"). Yet with the growing adoption of TV and increase in musical programming in the 1970s, Nabepro's dominance was ripped out from under them.

The show that did most to shake things up and went on to define a decade of Japanese pop was *Star Tanjou!* (*A Star is Born!*). First airing in 1971, *Star Tanjou!* launched the careers of the three solo singers Masako Mori, Junko Sakurada, and the incomparably wonderful Momoe Yamaguchi. These three singers were known collectively as *Hana no Chūsan Trio*, which translates clumsily into English as the "Lovely Trio of Third-Year Middle School Students". *Star Tanjou!* completely changed the way Japanese stars were produced and promoted – no more long apprenticeships on the tour circuit: stars were born on TV now. Megastars that emerged from *Star Tanjou!* in the 1970s and 1980s included Pink Lady, Hiromi Iwasaki, Akina Nakamori and Kyoko Koizumi.

Star Tanjou! succeeded in breaking the control of Watanabe Productions, but the show did not make pop music any less manipulative. The new talent agencies like Hori Production and Sun Music shared the *Star Tanjou!* winners out amongst themselves in a series of back-room deals that had little or nothing to do with what the singers themselves wanted. The songwriters themselves, on the other hand, were often more sensitive to the singers' situations. Throughout the 1970s and some of the 1980s, a kind of balance of power existed between the creative and business sides of the pop industry, with many artists forming fruitful partnerships with the songwriting teams assigned to them.

Momoe Yamaguchi began her career working predominantly with lyricist Kazuya Senka and songwriter Junichi Tokura, who produced songs like *Aoi Kajitsu* and *Hito Natsu no Keiken* that, while marvellous songs, scaled almost Serge Gainsbourg levels of ephebophilic sexual suggestiveness, before the teenage Yamaguchi reorientated her music towards songs that positioned her as a stronger and more independent character via the team of Yōkō Aki and Ryūdō Uzaki.

Another great female singer of this period was Saori Minami, whose agency eagerly positioned her as what has become regarded by some as the first idol singer in the modern Japanese sense of the word: as a produced singer marketed specifically on her cuteness, rather than simply an idol in the sense of being idolised. Nonetheless her songwriting team, consisting of lyricist Mieko Arima and songwriter Kyōhei Tsutsumi, managed to work with the singer to create a catalogue of magnificent pop tunes matched by few others of the period.

The aforementioned Pink Lady was a duo with a neat line in goofy dances and a scandalously long legged, more sexually mature image, but again their songs were top notch, with lyricist Yū Aku probably the greatest wordsmith in the history of Japanese pop. Bad girl singers like Linda Yamamoto and the peerlessly beautiful Chiyo Okumura also produced some of their best work in the early 1970s. While I've focused on female singers here, male singers like Hiromi Gō and Hideki Saijō had more than a few tunes to share between them. In the world of 1970s pop, however, the boys were generally not as playful or innovative as the ladies.

My pick for the best pop act of the 1970s would be the Candies. The all-girl trio was formed in 1972 by the fading Watanabe Productions. The Candies featured the songwriting talents of Michio Yamagami and Kōichi Morita, and then later Yūsuke Hoguchi and Kazuya Senka (who had worked with Momoe Yamaguchi). The vocalists enjoyed the rarity of a single backing band who played with them throughout most of their career. Accomplished artists in their own right, the backup musicians for the Candies had a second career as the progressive rock band Spectrum. The result of this collaboration is a run of singles between 1973 and 1978 that were all solid gold pop gems, containing a level of musicianship tighter and more consistent than any of the group's peers.

The nature of the pop industry started to undergo another shift as Japan entered the 1980s, and this had a knock-on effect on the musicianship it fostered. Advertising companies began to take greater control of the idol production industry, and the monolithic, monopolising advertising firm Dentsu emerged as a key player. Dentsu's stroke of genius was to bypass the talent show model and to introduce idols via appearances in commercials, which could be used to raise the profile of stars and sell them back to TV as performers, actresses and variety show personalities. Since the new idols only had about 15-30 seconds to first impress, their cute mannerisms became exaggerated and their musical aptitude wasn't particularly important. Unlike the prior generation of idols who were required by the TV performance format to more or less be able to sing, the newer 1980s idols were selected less for skill than for cuteness.

Bypassing the talent show format meant that a poor singer's voice could be fixed in the studio or simply replaced with another girl's voice. Moreover, changes in music technology, in particular the growing importance of synthesisers, meant that audiences no longer had the same expectations of seeing a live band or orchestra performing with the singers on TV. In the 1980s, artifice ruled and Seiko Matsuda was the undisputed star of the era.

Every bit as famous for her TV commercials as she was for her music, Seiko Matsuda epitomises the economics of 1980s pop music. Even if some contemporaries had better songs than Matsuda, as an icon – as an idol – Matsuda was and remains unsurpassable. Tellingly, her stage name combined two top brand names of the 1980s (Seiko watches and Matsuda/Mazda cars), and as something of a brand herself, Matsuda has enjoyed unprecedented staying power. In 1986 she shocked the nation by daring to have a baby and continue her career, rather than retire into graceful, obedient motherhood. More "serious" singers like Yumi Arai/Matsutoya had already done this, but idols exist in the front line of the battle over what constitute Japanese feminine values, and Matsuda's decision moved the front forward for women.

This positive step for women ran parallel with a sometimes exuberant and sometimes downright disturbing sauciness in pop music. Kyoko Koizumi's idol persona had an edge of panty-flashing impropriety to it, while the group Onyanko Club made a name for themselves with occasionally great songs like *Sailor Fuku wo Nugasanaide* (*Don't Make Me Take off My School Uniform*), *Otto! Chikan* (*Uh-oh! Pervert*) and *Oyoshi ni Natte Teacher* (*Be Good, Teacher!*). These songs acted as beacons for sexual harassment with a clear "no means yes" message.

With their sexualized innocence, Onyanko Club were an interchangeable mass idol collective produced by a young television executive called Yasushi Akimoto. With more than fifty members rotating into Onyanko Club over their two-year career, they were the ultimate idol group. But Idol music had started to sound dated. Change was afoot – change that would again be driven by a combination of underground talent and industry cash.

PUNK

When change comes to the pop industry in Japan, it tends to come in periods of technology-driven industry upheaval. The musical ideas still need to come from somewhere though, and a lively underground is where those ideas are fostered and develop. The 1970s was a boom period for pop music, but it was also a period of music industry consolidation around the cultural change wrought by the 1960s and the technological change of widespread TV ownership. Cracks in the system had opened up, so the industry had forged understandings with TV companies and the hippies to plug them. *Plus ça change, plus c'est la même chose.*

Radical politics had informed much of the late-1960s rebellion, but it imploded in the early 1970s, under pressure both from within and from authorities. Extremist incidents like the Lod Airport Massacre, the *Asama-Sansō* hostage crisis and the aforementioned Fukuoka Airport hijacking tarnished the image of youth politics as hypocritically violent. Meanwhile, the government cracked down on anything that looked even remotely left wing. With a broken spine, even anti-establishment underground music had been neutered and rendered irrelevant to most people.

One important music genre to emerge in the 1970s underground was progressive rock. In the UK, "prog rock" was one of the bêtes noires of the nascent punk scene, but in Japan no such distinction existed. Japanese underground music was living in the ruins of a youth culture crushed under the jackboot of police oppression and the kind of progressive rock that it produced, like Les Rallizes Dénudés, was something darker and more brutal than the fiddly synths and elves-and-goblins escapism of British prog's sillier purveyors. This is key to understanding contemporary Japanese alternative music: no ideological distinction exists between progressive rock and punk. One flows naturally into the other and they continue to interact comfortably to this day.

So the background for punk was in place with an experimental underground already probing the brutal extremes of feedback and noise, and rock'n'roll bands like Sonhouse who had devised a proto-punk DIY ethos of their own from the wreckage of the 1960s. With a thriving rock and pop mainstream above, a gap had opened up for something new and challenging to launch an attack from beneath, and all it needed was a trigger.

Pretty much from the moment The Ramones and The Damned started releasing records in the US and UK, there were Japanese bands importing and drawing inspiration from them. Through bands like Ultra Bide in Kyoto and Totsuzen Danball in Tokyo, Japan wasn't slow to get with punk. But partly because of the porous borders between the 1970s avant-garde scene and punk, picking the first Japanese punk band is a self-defeating exercise. Possibly the most important of this first generation, however, was Friction.

Instrumental in getting Japanese punk off the ground, Friction had had direct exposure during a stay in New York, where members played in bands like The Contortions and Teenage Jesus & The Jerks. Friction were also rooted in experimental 1970s Japanese outfits like ○△□ (pronounced: *Maru Sankaku Shikaku*).

Two of Japanese punk's founding scriptures, the 1979 compilation albums *Tokyo Rockers* and *Tokyo New Wave '79*, serve as a useful introduction to punk in Tokyo. The bands nowadays bracketed under the heading "Tokyo Rockers" usually include all the bands from the eponymous compilation (Friction, Mister Kite, Lizard, Mirrors, and S-Ken) as well as most of the *Tokyo New Wave '79* bands (Sex, Jisatsu, Pain, 8 1/2, Bolsie). In addition to the bands on the compilations, Gunjogacrayon, Saboten (not to be confused with the awful 2000s pop-punk band of the same name), Totsuzen Danball and early work by Jagatara also fit loosely under the "Rockers" banner.

While the *Tokyo Rockers* and *Tokyo New Wave '79* compilations were both released on major labels, the DIY spirit of the punk era also led to the appearance of the first indie labels such as Telegraph and Pass Records in Tokyo, as well as the short-lived Unbalance and *Rock Magazine*-afflilated Vanity labels in Osaka.

Inspired by the Tokyo scene, the Kansai area – of Osaka, Kyoto and Kobe – developed a swift riposte, which gave us Ultra Bide, Aunt Sally, SS and the magnificent Inu. From these bands, artists like Phew and Hijokaidan sprang out. Meanwhile, the city of Nagoya developed its own punk scene with key figures including The Star Club, who later gave birth to Genbaku Onanies.

While the Tokyo Rockers were essentially art-punks and hard rock outfits, often with roots in the 1970s avant-garde scene and inspired by the early New York and UK punk scenes, punk diversified in the 1980s. Harder-edged bands like The Stalin, G.I.S.M., Gauze, Kikeiji, Laughin' Nose and Masturbation offered their own fiercer takes on punk, mixing it with metal and edging towards hardcore. Similarly, the noise scene that emerged in Kyoto and Osaka around the Drugstore experimental music space and Alchemy Records label was undoubtedly influenced by punk, but again took inspiration from experimental 1970s underground music, which led to some of the most fearsome and dangerous acts of the era. Against Hijokaidan's cascade of blood, piss and vomit, Hanatarash competed for who could get banned from the most venues by taking industrial tools and machetes to their instruments, stage sets, and on at least one occasion, a dead cat. Eye Yamantaka and Mitsuru Tabata from Hanatarash went on to form the Boredoms, with Tabata then moving on to Tokyo's Zeni Geva. Less theatrical but in many ways more sonically radical acts like Hijokaidan member Toshiji Mikawa's Incapacitants and Tokyo-based artist Masami Akita's Merzbow helped consolidate this experimentalism into what became known as "noise". At the same time, Tokyo bands like Aburadako and Ruins were also advancing in a more experimental direction, taking underground music further away from both punk and 1970s new rock, and creating Japanese precursors to post-hardcore and math rock.

Punk was expanding its poppier extremes as well, with Shonen Knife reconfiguring punk as naive pop. Meanwhile, the frankly overrated but nonetheless wildly popular Blue Hearts helped lay the foundations for a sanitised version of punk that sees it through the filter of nostalgic youthful abandon, and were vitally important in making punk work in the mainstream.

The link to the mainstream is also important in understanding punk's cleaner-cut, better-connected sibling new wave, which carried the baton for a certain thread of art-pop creativity through from the 1970s to the 1990s.

NEW WAVE

In addition to the rock'n'roll and underground bands of the 1970s, there were also popular artists who didn't really fit into any particular niche, some of whom were to have a lasting influence on the emergence of new wave. Happy End, despite only making three albums, are regularly cited as the most influential Japanese band of all time, and ex-members went on to shine with subsequent projects. Sadistic Mika Band and RC Succession were also important bands of that era, and among other things brought elements of glam rock from the UK into the Japanese rockosphere. The visual aesthetic of glam in particular would have a powerful influence on the development of new wave.

Happy End's Haruomi Hosono and Sadistic Mika Band drummer Yukihiro Takashi joined up with keyboard player Ryūichi Sakamoto to form Yellow Magic Orchestra (YMO) in 1977. While composer Isao Tomita had been an important pioneer of electronic music in Japan, YMO helped to normalise the idea of technopop and opened up the mainstream to the idea of the synth as the lead instrument. While not strictly a new wave band, coming as they did from an entirely mainstream background, YMO inhabited a role in relation to the punk and new wave scenes rather similar to that of Brian Eno in the West. For example, aside from writing YMO records, member Hosono took on the difficult task of making Fukuoka rockers Sheena & The Rokkets into something a major label could handle, while Sakamoto produced early music by Friction and worked with Kansai punk-poet Phew.

When genuine new wave acts started to emerge, inspired by the DIY ethos of punk and the explosion of British and American bands like Talking Heads, XTC, Devo and more, it was a small world where things took off quickly. Influential in this nascent Tokyo new wave scene, Hikashu vocalist Koichi Makigami recalls: "I had just started Hikashu," he explains, "My friend Haruo Chikada had a radio programme that broadcast at 2 AM. I made a demo tape and went to hand it to him at his station, explaining about the music, 'We don't have a drummer: we're a rhythm box band.' Then a guy who was waiting over in the corner says, 'Hey, me too. I'm doing the same kind of band.' It turns out this was Hajime Tachibana from the Plastics."

The short-lived but influential Plastics, along with P-Model and Hikashu, were very important in popularising the term "technopop" and driving the emergence of synth-based music as a contemporary phenomenon. While Hikashu are probably the best band in the history of Japanese music, other artists in a related vein were Halmens, who had graduated to new wave from the earlier postpunk band Shonen Homeruns, and the magnificent Chakra, who combined cutting-edge synthesiser technology with melodies that merged new wave with Japanese and Okinawan folk music.

Music aside, identification with artists in Japan was just as much a tribal marker as it was about melodies. In the early 1980s, punks and new wavers created their own tribes, with punk sprouting a neofascist, skinhead subculture with connections to the yakuza, Japanese nationalists and various new religious cults (a trend that Ultra Bide founder Hide Fujiwara claims drove him to abandon Japan for New York for sixteen years). A particularly odd subculture also sprang up around the label Nagomu Records, founded by Kera of new wave band Uchoten. Nagomu bands attracted a legion of obsessive fangirls with their own eclectic and diverse fashion ethos that took punk's attitude of throwing together vintage clothes in a variety of styles, and added to that a desexualised, sometimes infantile style – an image of childhood extended to extremes. There are roots of the later gothic Lolita fashion styles in elements of this subculture, and distant echoes of it remain in the kind of cute/grotesque Harajuku fashion most famously exemplified by Kyary Pamyu Pamyu. Nevertheless, the "Nagomu Gals" were very much their own thing, with close ties to the label that closed in 1989.

The rise of Japanese punk and new wave provided a musical landscape that resembles current alternative and underground scenes. Interest in punk and new wave also facilitated the growth of infrastructure, a support network of independent record labels and concert venues. In the late 1970s, modern "live house" culture began to coalesce in Tokyo, with bands gathering into a circuit built around small clubs. The venue Shinjuku Loft (then in its old Nishi-Shinjuku location rather than its current home just down the road in Kabukicho) was vitally important as a crucible for the burgeoning punk scene, as was the S-Ken studio in Roppongi. *Tokyo Rockers* had been recorded at Loft, and Kenzo Saeki of Halmens and Pearl Kyodai says that the Loft event *Drive to 80s* was the first time audiences at shows had broken the tradition of sitting down to enjoy the music and instead had been forced by the crush of people in the overcrowded venue to stand up throughout the performance. This is probably an exaggeration, but these kinds of changes in underground live music culture were certainly happening on a large scale at this time.

The growth in the number and style of music venues had additional significance for the development of live music culture and infrastructure in Japan, though. Makigami again experienced this firsthand.

"Around the mid-80s so many bands and indie labels started to appear – we also made some records by ourselves, although it wasn't so cheap. In the 70s or the beginning of the 80s it was good for bands because live houses paid a guarantee and gave you food. Around the mid-80s, suddenly the bands had to pay. There used to be very few live houses – Loft, La Mama – but in the mid-80s so many bands appeared and live houses became like rental rooms. This was a big change. Before, 80% of venues would pay you; it was easy to get by with only playing music. From the mid-80s you couldn't live off music."

What Makigami is describing here is the influence of the so-called "band boom" that came about in the mid-80s. Not always specifically punk and new wave in style, this movement nevertheless grew out of the punk era's DIY ethos, and the flood of new bands helped cause a shift from a situation where artists would compete for paying gigs at a small number of venues to one where hundreds of venues offered gigs on a pay-to-play basis to whoever could bring in the crowds or afford the cost. This transformation of the live circuit is one that has left its mark on the structure of the music scene to this day.

The influence of the new wave era didn't just lie in Tokyo's grotty live basements though. New wave also began to infiltrate – and allow itself to be co-opted by – the mainstream. Juicy Fruits (driven by Makigami's friend Haruo Chikada) were an early example of what was sometimes called *techno-kayo* (i.e. *kayōkyoku* with technopop arrangements). Chakra's Mishio Ogawa took her distinctive voice solo with moderate success, while Halmens members Jun Togawa and Maki Nomiya both became stars on the fringes of the mainstream. Miharu Koshi, who had emerged out of the tail end of "new music", teamed up with YMO's Haruomi Hosono and went fully new wave. Former Plastics keyboard player Masahide Sakuma, Halmens' Kenzo Saeki and YMO's Akiko Yano all worked with 80s idol Kyoko Koizumi, while pre-recorded synth-based backing tracks began to replace live bands in idol performances.

Ideas from idol music also flowed in reverse back into the avant-garde. Former new wave singer Jun Togawa took elements of idol imagery, twisted them to support a more critical agenda, and then threw them back in the audience's face. At the same time, the pop industry was now influenced at a fundamental level by demands of advertising agencies, which made the idol-industrial complex openly and extravagantly artificial. In response to the growing artificiality of pop music (and culture in its broader sense), new wave bands like the Plastics both celebrated and satirised the cultural trend towards superficiality. As a result, the mainstream and underground sides of the music industry spectrum, despite different motivations, ended up working towards similar creative ends – if you're ironically plastic or plastic for real, you're still helping define the era in terms of the same notions of artificiality and mass production in culture.

THE DEATH OF IDOLS AND KAYŌKYOKU

By the late 1980s, *kayōkyoku* had run out of steam. It had driven itself so far into the blind alley of idol music that the two were inseparable, and new things were starting to appear that would set the stage for the next big shift in the Japanese music scene. It's in many ways a fascinating period for mainstream pop, with more and more artists and producers casting about, aware that the next big thing is on its way and desperately hoping to be on the crest of the wave when it comes.

Chisato Moritaka is one of the more interesting singers to emerge from this late 1980s period, with her early material embracing synthpop in its arrangements while at the same time harking back to the 1970s by covering songs like Saori Minami's *17-sai*. Similarly, Moritaka's image combined typically idol-ish puffy dresses with sharper colour schemes, elements of 1980s "power dressing", and legs that went on for miles. She was rooted in *kayōkyoku* and idol music, but her image was far from either style, and really it wouldn't be until the K-Pop explosion of 2011 that Japan would see another star like her.

A pop duo called Wink appeared in 1988, with music that borrowed heavily from the sort of Stock, Aitken & Waterman production style then popular in the UK, having one of their biggest hits with a Japanese cover of Kylie Minogue's *Turn it into Love*. Again synthpop arrangements proliferated alongside elements of idol style, although Wink's big thing was that they didn't smile very often. It sounds silly, and looking at their videos now, it's clear that they actually smiled a perfectly normal amount, but in the heavily micromanaged world of 1980s pop, even small deviations from formula were shocking. The way Wink took dance-influenced pop music and presented it with a sort of blank insouciance predicted the popularity of Perfume in the 2000s.

Wink, like Chisato Moritaka, were selling records at a time of change in the Japanese music market. One change was precipitated by the discovery of an unexpected audience for Eurobeat by entrepreneur Masato "Max" Matsuura, who founded the company Avex in 1988. A second was the emergence of the 1980s "band boom", partly documented by the fondly remembered TV audition show *Ikasu Band Tengoku*, more often abbreviated to *Ikaten!*

I spoke with indie rocker Kentaro Nakao about the TV show, which he watched as a teenager.

"Most of the bands were just comical and seemed happy to be on there just once," Nakao recalls, "but the bands I identified with from the show had a different attitude. Blankey Jet City were the one that made the biggest impression on me, even if their music was quite different from what I was into. I appreciated bands who didn't seem to be trying to appeal to the critics, the viewers or me – whoever it was."

Nakao, like many of his peers, was drawn to a cooler, less

obviously manufactured image. At around the same time in the late 80s and early 90s, bands like Spitz and Unicorn were establishing themselves as influential bands who brought a high degree of artistry to their music, often with strong 60s influences sitting alongside some roots in the aftermath of punk. For those willing to take a step into something weirder, former Nagomu band Tama offered an eccentric and distinctly Japanese take on rock and pop songwriting that would also have a powerful if slow-burning influence. Even in fully mainstream pop, a less affected, more casual and loose seeming image would be a part of what defined Japanese pop for the next ten years.

However, if we must pick one single moment that defines the passing of the idol/*kayōkyoku* era, then it is the day in November 1989 when the song *Precious Heart* failed to become Seiko Matsuda's 25th successive number one single. She conceded that place to *Gravity of Love* by a songwriter and producer named Tetsuya Komuro.

J-POP AND THE BIRTH OF CONTEMPORARY JAPANESE MUSIC

The style that came to be the defining term for modern Japanese pop, and the style with which the producer Tetsuya Komuro was to be inexorably linked, was J-Pop. It was originally coined by the radio station J-Wave as a way of marketing the new band-based popular music that was emerging at the end of the 1980s, and – for all the horrors it has inflicted since – it was a form born in several key ways out of punk and new wave. In its initial incarnation, J-Pop's musical identity was defined by three key producers and artists.

J-Pop producer Tetsuya Komuro made a name for himself in the 1980s as a member of TM Network. The group had started out as a synth-based new wave band before evolving into fairly appalling stadium rockers whose enduring popularity rested largely on the misty-eyed nostalgia of thirtysomethings and the fact that they did the theme song to the anime *City Hunter*. Komuro, the band's keyboard player, had also developed a successful solo career alongside the band, and he was considered the ideal candidate to help the Eurobeat-based Avex label go beyond distribution and start producing local Japanese acts that would take dance music to a wider local audience. Komuro produced and wrote songs for countless hit-making Avex artists, including TRF, Tomomi Kahala, Ami Suzuki, Namie Amuro and his own new band Globe. His style of tinny dance-pop remains one of the most characteristic and recognisable sounds of the 90s.

If the dance-pop side of J-Pop was defined by Komuro over at Avex, the rock side was deeply coloured by the work of Takeshi Kobayashi. He was a producer and songwriter with obvious 60s and classic rock influences informing his music more than punk and new wave, but as a 90s producer of the band Mr. Children, his work still stands as a link between the new wave and J-Pop eras. An archetypal late 80s "band boom" act, Mr. Children updated mainstream Japanese rock with new wave influences, in particular Elvis Costello, and along with Kobayashi they went onto define the sound of Japanese rock in the 90s. Mr. Children never made anything worth listening to after 1997's *Bolero* but it didn't matter: their work had been done. Their producer, Kobayashi, moonlighted briefly as a hitmaker with the band My Little Lover, whose short, three-album run (*Evergreen, Presents, New Adventure*) between 1995 and 1998 is perhaps the definitive document of the late-1990s J-Pop band sound, and notably superior to similar bands like Every Little Thing and Dreams Come True.

In contrast to other hugely successful 1990s groups, Judy And Mary were a punk-pop band, largely manufactured by Sony Music but who were nevertheless a self-contained songwriting and performing unit. Working throughout their career with producer Masahide Sakuma, formerly of new wave/technopop pioneers the Plastics, Judy And Mary defined the format of kooky-girl-singer-and-some-guys that would go on to become the standard formula for pretty much all punk-influenced major label bands into the new millennium. Nevertheless, Judy And Mary were also really good. The band's baroque guitar lines alongside vocalist Yuki Isoya's charisma and their imaginative, formula-defying song arrangements meant that Judy And Mary were that rarest of beasts: a genuinely original band who were also really popular.

While Komuro, Judy And Mary, and Kobayashi were three key driving influences of the J-Pop era, there were many more, all making sales that would seem insane by modern standards. Acts like B'z, Glay, Zard, Speed, Misia, The Brilliant Green, Puffy, Max, SMAP, Kinki Kids, The Yellow Monkey, Spitz, Sharam Q, Hitomi, Chara, Luna Sea, L'Arc en Ciel, and more were all selling in the millions, and some of them were even quite good.

J-Pop remained vibrant because it was, initially at least, an artist-led phenomenon, and for all the clumsiness of some of the attempted appropriations from overseas (Tetsuya Komuro's hilarious attempt at drum'n'bass on Yuki Uchida's *Only You* is a case in point), at least the artists were listening. Maybe paradoxically, J-Pop also has embedded in its name a reversal of the association the term "*kayōkyoku*" had with alien "Western-style" music, replaced by an embrace of pop's native Japaneseness. Coincidental perhaps, but there is a neat symbolism in how the growth of J-Pop has gone hand in hand with a decline in the market share of foreign artists in Japan. As far as Japanese audiences were concerned, J-Pop was rendering foreign music unnecessary.

And the sales figures bands were racking up in the late 90s really do defy contemporary imagination. Today a chart-topping single might sell about 100,000 in its first week. In the late 90s, sales of over a million were par for the course – some idol groups like AKB48 can hit those levels today, but only by using promotion gimmicks to encourage fans to make multiple purchases of the same CD. In 2011 AKB48 sold about 850,000 copies of their dreadful album *Koko wa Ita Koto*, but in 1997 Mr. Children's *Bolero* sold double that in its first week. In fact, in 1997, AKB48's album would have come in at number 26 in the yearly rankings, between Mayo Okamoto's *Smile* and Toshinobu Kubota's *La La La Love Thang*. In 1998 AKB48 wouldn't have even made the top 30.

SHIBUYA-*KEI* AND JAPAN DISCOVERS INDIE

So how was the underground doing in the 90s? Pretty well as it turns out, and the main reason for that was Shibuya-*kei*.

The origins of Shibuya-*kei* aren't easy to define, but as with J-Pop, it has some roots in punk and especially new wave. Pizzicato Five debuted in 1985 with the *Audrey Hepburn Complex* EP, produced by YMO's (formerly Happy End's) Haruomi Hosono. In 1990, the group was joined by vocalist Maki Nomiya, formerly of new wave bands Halmens and Portable Rock. Pizzicato Five's music has obvious links in its early days to new wave-era technopop, although it also draws on '60s pop traditions and elements of bossa nova that would later come to define the sound of Shibuya-*kei*.

Another precursor of Shibuya-*kei* is sometimes suggested as the style known as "city pop". Again heavily influenced by Hosono – this time his work with Happy End – city pop was self-consciously sophisticated pop music drawing on jazz and 60s pop in a similar fashion to the way Shibuya-*kei* later would. Singers like Akira Terao and Tatsuro Yamashita are often associated with the style, as well as some idol singers like Momoko Kikuchi and Miho Nakayama. Basically any 80s albums with pictures of swimming pools on the front are probably city pop.

One key difference between city pop and Shibuya-*kei* was that while city pop was essentially a mainstream pop/rock phenomenon extruding from the "new music" tradition, Shibuya-*kei* was fundamentally indie. It was music made by and for record store nerds, and that brings us to perhaps its most important influence: British indie label Él Records.

Él Records was set up by Mike Alway under the aegis of Cherry Red, releasing artists like The Monochrome Set, Simon Turner, Momus, the Would-Be-Goods, Bad Dream Fancy Dress and Vic Godard. Él Records cultivated a musical and visual aesthetic built around stylised 60s fashion and pop art sophistication, and a dry, subversive sense of humour. The label may never have been a big commercial success in the UK, but its aesthetic struck a chord with record collectors in Japan, and was a big influence on the Shibuya-*kei* band Flipper's Guitar.

Flipper's Guitar, a duo of Keigo Oyamada and Kenji Ozawa, are probably the most important act in the development of Shibuya-*kei*. The three albums they made between 1989 and 1991 set the tone for a lot of what was to come, combining 1980s British guitar pop with dance music, jazz, and an increasingly cut-and-paste approach to song construction. After the end of Flipper's Guitar, Kenji Ozawa became a star in his own right, while bandmate Keigo Oyamada adopted the nom de rock Cornelius and started the Trattoria label. Trattoria was influential in promoting overseas artists like The Pastels, Apples in Stereo and Louis Philippe, as well as a broad range of Japanese alternative music from noise acts like Violent Onsen Geisha (*Bōryoku Onsen Geisha*) to the outright pop of Kahimi Karie.

The eclecticism of Shibuya-*kei* made it difficult to define, even for the artists who found themselves sometimes unexpectedly associated with it. Aiha Higurashi explained in an interview for this book that her formative musical experiences had been in the hardcore scene of the mid-80s, and her band Seagull Screaming Kiss Her Kiss Her had debuted at a Guitar Wolf show, yet as the 90s progressed, she found herself on Trattoria.

"Keigo Oyamada was a huge name with Trattoria, and of course Kahimi Karie – they were super-popular," Higurashi explains, "People around them named it 'Shibuya-*kei*', but the musicians themselves didn't actually know until later that that was what it was called. My band is what's called '*ura*-Shibuya-*kei*', a kind of 'death-Shibuya-*kei*'. We're not candy-poppy, we were more edgy than Kahimi Karie, with her super-cute vocals and dancing. I'm a fan of Kahimi Karie and I like her, but we were totally different. Within that label we were always alone."

The diverse groups on the Trattoria label included influential indie acts, but they also crossed over into the mainstream. A major hit was Kahimi Karie's song *Good Morning World*, which had been written and produced for Trattoria by Él Records alumnus Momus. Perhaps Shibuya-*kei*'s defining hit, with its whispered vocals, 60s horns, an psychedelic Soft Machine samples, it's also significant as almost certainly the first and last time a song lyrically referencing British postpunk band The Fall will make the top ten of the Japanese singles charts.

With its fusion of 60s music, jazz and sophisticated modern pop sheen, Shibuya-*kei* shared many elements with the earlier genre of city pop. Shibuya-*kei* also incorporated elements from bossa nova, 80s UK indie guitar pop, house music and the late-80s Manchester scene. If there can be said to be a core Shibuya-*kei* sound, it lies somewhere in that combination of influences. A look at the Trattoria "menu" of the 1990s reveals far more than that though, with the avant-garde noise of Violent Onsen Geisha, the off-kilter synthpop of Takako Minekawa and the lo-fi garage rock of Seagull Screaming Kiss Her Kiss Her. These arty Trattoria acts sat alongside more poppy performers like Kahimi Karie and Hideki Kaji. The broader scene was no less varied, incorporating everything from the quirky electronic pop of Fantastic Plastic Machine to the psychedelic, Krautrock-influenced spacerock of Buffalo Daughter.

So how did something so eclectic and often downright anti-commercial become so popular? One reason is economics. There was lots of money around in the 1990s and major labels were willing to take a chance on weirder sounds on the off chance some of it might pay off. At the same time, record shops in Japan, particularly Shibuya's music superstores like Tower Records and HMV, tended to give a lot of power to the buyers of individual stores to select and promote music they liked. A lot of Shibuya-*kei*'s early success was driven by cultural curators, record shop staff, and influential label owners – like Trattoria's Oyamada – deciding what was going to be cool, and passing down their decrees in a model very similar to the way the fashion industry worked.

In fact, in the end, Shibuya-*kei* makes more sense as a fashion phenomenon than a musical one. There were genuine musical scenes in the 1990s like the Shimo-Kitazawa indie rock scene that gave us bands like Fishman's and Sunny Day Service, and the "Tokyo New Wave of New Wave" scene that gave us Polysics, Motocompo, Skyfisher and Spoozys, but with Shibuya-*kei* the music itself was all over the place, and the main thing linking it together was the sense of style and aesthetics. Many of its most recognisable icons were models like Maki Nomiya and Kahimi Karie, or people like the photographer Hiromix who exist in a cross-media world. Shibuya-*kei* owed a lot of its vitality to its position as a fashion movement, and the one constant of fashion is that it changes.

THE END OF JAPANESE MUSIC HISTORY AND THE BIRTH OF THE ETERNAL NOW

In the late 90s, mainstream Japanese pop was at the pinnacle of its commercial might. Indie music had also been undergoing a boom of sorts, but by the early 2000s, a lot of that energy was starting to dissipate.

The biggest stars of the late 90s J-Pop la la land were Hikaru Utada and Ayumi Hamasaki. The R&B-influenced Utada's 1999 debut album *First Love* remains the biggest selling album in Japanese music history, and was also a landmark in the shifting taste of audiences away from the tinny Eurobeat of Tetsuya Komuro and towards a lusher, richer sound. At the same time, the prolific output of the chameleonic Hamasaki made her Japan's most consistently successful female artist of the era (and perhaps ever). Artists like these were making such absurd profits for labels, talent agencies and advertisers that for the next ten years the music industry was in a state of paralysis, releasing the same kind of music over and over again to steadily diminishing returns.

In the late 90s, J-Pop had run out of ideas and there was now nothing new waiting in the wings to replace it. Nor was there urgency for change at the top. The mainstream was about to enter a long period of commercial and creative atrophy. After the turn of the millennium, the Trattoria label ground to a halt and with no centre to hold Shibuya-*kei*'s already diverse collection of artists together, the threads snapped and it flew apart. The music didn't disappear: Shibuya-*kei* simply ceased to exist as a viable marketing bracket. Bands like Quruli, Supercar and Number Girl had appeared and shown a different, more immediate, more thrilling way to be cool, and the marketing money had migrated towards them in search of the hot new thing.

The biggest changes of the new millennium would not be a top-down imposition of pop culture by elites, but rather it would be driven by subcultures. The late 90s saw idol music rebound, driven this time by the *otaku* (largely male, obsessive fan) subculture. The mass idol collective Morning Musume, modelled partly on Onyanko Club, achieved breakout fame with the 1999 hit *Love Machine*, which set the stage for two decades of idol dominance. Meanwhile, the "gyaru" girls' subculture was driving the successes of stars like Ayumi Hamasaki.

Subcultures were gradually asserting dominance over the musical landscape, while television and radio were losing their power to influence public tastes. Nevertheless, the same basic network of major labels, talent agencies and advertising agencies controlled the infrastructure. Venues of the sort that had hosted the punk scene, the late 80s band boom, the 90s new wave revival and Shimo-Kitazawa indie rock scene were still expanding all over Tokyo and the rest of Japan. This was the Japan I arrived in when I stepped off the plane in 2001, with J-Pop coming down gradually from its dizzying late 90s highs and indie music working out a new direction for itself after the fading of Shibuya-*kei*'s light.

PART 3:

THE ECONOMIC, POLITICAL, AND PRACTICAL
PERILS OF THE GIGGING ARTIST, OR HOW NOT
TO QUIT YOUR BAND

KOENJI, TOKYO

I venture down a dingy staircase at the back of a building on Koenji's Pal shopping arcade, weaving past a crowd of punks with spiky hair and studded leather jackets. They're gathered around the entrance to a venue called Gear, but I keep on going down, deeper underground into the sub-basement venue of 20000V (Twenty-Thousand Volts). The walls of are layered inches thick with old flyers and posters, all covered with a film of grime, sweat and nonconformism. It's so punk that the guy at the door has the words "punk" and "rock" tattooed onto his knuckles. Drinks are only available if you buy tickets at the door and exchange them for alcohol at the counter. I'm not sure if this is entirely legal, but it adds to the sense of illicit pleasure.

Inside, a hyperactive goblin creature is using the stage as a climbing frame and barking what sounds to me like incomprehensible but surely profound and life-changing gibberish at the audience, against a backdrop of an off-the-wall new wave/postpunk band with a pair of duelling synths. They seem to be called The Hasshin Telepathies. A tightly-wound and ultimately explosive collision of motorik Kraut and Sonic Youth-style feedback and noise follows, delivered blankly by a trio of girls called Nisennenmondai, all three barely moving but for the drummer's flailing arms. There's a disarming sense of theatre in the way they position themselves onstage, facing each other in a triangle like a witches' coven as they create their wicked alchemy.

The final band of the night is The Warm, another synth-based new wave-influenced band. The name nods to The Normal's song Warm Leatherette *and the band are clearly heavily indebted to early Mute Records and other synth-based punk-era music, in particular the likes of DAF and Liaisons Dangereuses, but they balance it out with songs that are off-kilter pop masterclasses. For the first time in my life in Japan, I feel like I've found a place I belong.*

After moving to Tokyo in 2001, Koenji is where I first started to feel at home. The UFO Club at the Higashi-Koenji end of town was where I had my first taste of the garage and mod scene. I fell in love with a brilliant but rough-edged, early Kinks-like band called the Mookees as well as the irrepressibly energetic Do The Boogie (who later became the Fadeaways). I was kicked in the gut by dirty 60s-style garage rockers like The Acetones and The Outs and charmed by retro Showa-era pop revivalists Hanari Kyoko and the Snipers. However, while this scene was fascinating, it was also very restrict-ive. The mod side of the scene in particular treated music as an accessory to the wider construction of a fashion image that marked one's tribe. In this sense Tokyo's tribes were true to the ethos of their 60s forebears, but while 60s mods lived in their own moment and had the capacity to evolve – in occasionally spectacular ways with bands like The Who and The Creation – 21st-Century Japanese mods are lovingly preserved museum pieces and musically irrelevant.

The closely related garage scene in Tokyo has typically been better able to throw sonic curveballs while retaining its essentially retro nature. When garage band The 5,6,7,8's were riding high on the back of an appearance in the film *Kill Bill*, wild things were going on around them. Meanwhile, bands like the Saturns were dressing up in Wehrmacht infantry uniforms and making the scuzziest, most brutal sound imaginable in their five-minute sets.

It was the experimental side of Tokyo's underground music scene that ended up capturing my attention most fully though. Bands like Nisennenmondai led me to synth-punk trio The Warm and on to more wonderful postpunk-influenced bands like Elevation, Usagi Spiral A and Drive to the Forest in a Japanese Car; however, more important in the long run to my understanding of the scene were Panicsmile.

At first, I didn't really get Panicsmile. They were rhythmically unpredictable, wilfully atonal, and far outside any frame of reference I had at the time. If I'd paid better attention to Captain Beefheart in my youth, I might have been able to make sense of it, but my first listen left me baffled. Nevertheless, Panicsmile were a band I kept hearing about, who kept cropping up on bills that looked good, and they seemed to be deeply respected by pretty much everyone in the scene, so I persevered. More than anything else I experienced, getting into Panicsmile and finding a way into their appeal gave me an instinctive understanding of what the alternative scene at that time was about.

Although at that time based in Tokyo, Panicsmile formed in 1992 in the Fukuoka scene on the western island of Kyushu, which later gave us Number Girl. Number Girl's Kentaro Nakao told me, "The reason I moved to Fukuoka was because of Panicsmile. I had been living about an hour from Fukuoka in Kitakyushu, where there were lots of yakuza and hardcore kids sniffing paint thinner. I didn't want to get into that scene. I was an art student at the time and I met Yoshida from Panicsmile at university. Panicsmile had this concept of 'Hakata no wave'* and used to do an event called 'Chelsea Q' with these bands like Velocityut and Accidents in Too Large Field. These shows were tiny, went on all night, and they were crazy."

Panicsmile was founded on a principle borrowed from UK postpunk contrarians Wire of playing "anything but rock". Of course the term "rock" can be applied pretty loosely and many definitions would easily cover everything both Wire and Panicsmile have done over their careers, but in any case, there's an urge to push against convention that is embedded at the heart of their musical approach.

"Fukuoka at that time was all about *mentai* rock – bands like The Roosters and The Mods," recalls Nakao, "[Panicsmile's] Yoshida liked a lot of the music, but not the scene or its fan culture. Hakata no wave was about being anti that."

In many ways Panicsmile's career and that of Number Girl parallel each other. In addition to the anarchic Chelsea Q events, both bands also had early connections with the Fukuoka venue Vivre Hall, where Panicsmile leader Yoshida and Number Girl's

---

* Hakata no wave was named after Hakata, the main train station in Fukuoka. Hataka and Fukuoka are names that are often used interchangeably.

Kentaro Nakao and Hisako Tabuchi all spent time working. The venue was another key location for the development of the late 90s Fukuoka scene that was also home to bands like Mo'some Tonebender, Rumtag and the teenage Ringo Shiina. Both Panicsmile and Number Girl moved to Tokyo at roughly the same time, and both bands moved in the early 2000s from punk towards more rhythmically experimental music, with Panicsmile actually playing as Shutoku Mukai's backing band in some of his early post-Number Girl gigs, before his next band Zazen Boys became a fixed entity. Most importantly, both bands were incredibly influential in very different ways.

While Number Girl were stars who inspired thousands and whose music still now casts a shadow over the popular imagination of Japanese indie rock, Panicsmile embedded themselves in the underground scene. Panicsmile's Yoshida took up tenure as booking manager of the venue Akihabara Club Goodman, which gave him a powerful curatorial platform in the Tokyo alternative scene. In a nutshell, Panicsmile's influence was bottom-up whereas Number Girl's was top-down.

Making Club Goodman into a magnet for developing oddball young indie bands with an experimental tilt, Yoshida also helped bring them to wider attention through his Headache Sounds label, and later for the flawed but admirable Perfect Music and the more conventional P-Vine label. Many of the most thrilling bands emerging from the punk and indie basement venues in the mid-2000s had been influenced by Panicsmile at early stages in their development. Bands like Tacobonds, Worst Taste and The Mornings to name but three were all exciting, original acts in their own right, but they were also clearly products of the environment Yoshida had helped foster at Goodman. Panicsmile's rhythmically dense, tonally and harmonically unconventional anti-rock did more than anything else to help me unlock this world of clearly punk- and alt-rock-influenced music that had nonetheless taken a different evolutionary path from the bands I had grown up with in the UK.

Back across town in Koenji, the venue 20000V was serving as a lightning rod for the same kind of eccentric alt-rock musicians alongside its bread and butter of sweaty hardcore punk. There, bands like rockabilly new wave trance-punk duo Kirihito and later the Boredoms-influenced heavy junk noise of Groundcover. (the full stop is part of the name: don't ask) helped to define the venue's identity as a dirtier, scuzzier, louder mirror of the cleaner-edged Club Goodman. Connections between the two venues remain strong to this day, with bands and staff from Goodman and 20000V (now relocated and officially known as Ni-man Den-atsu) collaborating on projects and events like the Tokyo Boredom noise rock festival.

There was more to Koenji Tokyo's music scene than discord and noise though.

Occasionally crossing over into its rough-edged and uncompromising counterpart, there was a poppier, more new wave-influenced thread of alternative music.

My entry point here was through the band Mosquito, who I had met at the Koenji Showboat in my days of stalking The Students. As a group who combined dissonance with disarmingly chirpy pop influences, often ricocheting wildly between the two extremes within the space of a single song, their tastes were very eclectic. They were representative of a kind of band with a clear pop sensibility who had nonetheless honed their sound in a live culture where experimental musical ideas were thoroughly normalised.

Through Mosquito, I discovered the delightfully demented violin-led chiptune/hip hop (chip-hop?) duo Miami as well as the more guitar-based but equally off-the-wall (and beautifully named) Shoot My Disco. An important influence for many of these groups was the band Boat (usually stylised BOaT with a typically Japanese disregard to syntax), who had made a name for themselves in the late 1990s with a playful mix of indie rock and progressive pop. Members of Boat had gone on to form the post-rock band Natsumen, who occupied a similarly highly regarded position somewhere between pop and the avant-garde. It was also through bands like Mosquito that I also came to discover the late 90s "Tokyo new wave of new wave" scene.

Now being British, the term "new wave of new wave" always meant to me bands like These Animal Men, Elastica and the whole proto-Britpop Fierce Panda Records scene circa 1993. In Japan, the term relates to the bands featured on and associated with the *Tokyo New Wave of New Wave '98* compilation on the now defunct Tinstar Records (or "TiNSTAR" in the scene's creative syntax).

The core sound of *Tokyo New Wave of New Wave '98* was a revival of the late 70s/early 80s sound epitomised by P-Model and the Plastics, with bands like Motocompo, Spoozys and Polysics leading the way, but its origins were a bit more diverse than that. Members of Spoozys and Chicago Bass had roots in the fading Shibuya-*kei* scene. The compilation also featured the fantastic Skyfisher who, sounding like a fiercer, more political Polysics, were leading representatives of the new wave revival's Chiba prefectural division.

For this "new wave of new wave", the career of Polysics resembled that of Number Girl; both groups did a couple of indie releases but were quickly picked up by a major labels – Toshiba EMI in Number Girl's case, Sony's indie-ish Ki/oon imprint in the case of Polysics. The bands differed, however, insofar as Polysics' new wave revival was tied to the past and lacked a broad influence on fans and other musicians at the grassroots level. Despite an early association with the venue Shinjuku JAM, the new wave revival had no real home base, and even with the efforts of people like Nobuya Usui of Motocompo and Takashi Nakayama of Skyfisher – with their Poplot and Labsick labels respectively – there was no one really able to take on the sort of curatorial roles that had helped propel Shibuya-*kei* into the mainstream or which was sustaining the network of underground venues used by Number Girl's followers.

What seemed to happen with the new wave revival in the end was that the rock and punk side slowly gravitated towards the contemporary alt-rock scene at places like Club Goodman, while the cutesier technopop side linked up with the evolving offspring of Shibuya-*kei*. Out of this came the frenetic sugar rush of the Usagi-Chang label, the colour splash of Vroom Sound Records, and the more consciously post-Shibuya-*kei* Softly! Records. A quick infodump of artists that emerged from this scene would include Flipper's Guitar soundalikes the Aprils, the eclectic and dizzyingly high octane nonsense of Eel, the 8-bit jazz-pop of YMCK, ever-evolving pop princess Hazel Nuts Chocolate (now known simply as HNC) and the hyperactive cut-and-paste genius of Plus-tech Squeeze Box. Also associated with this scene at the time was a young duo from Kanazawa called Capsule, whose chief songwriter Yasutaka Nakata would later go on to become the most celebrated producer of his era and the man behind electro-idol trio Perfume and fashion icon/popstar Kyary Pamyu Pamyu.

It's easy to look at the 90s, see people like Kahimi Karie in the top ten, and say that it was a golden age that has since passed, but the music never went anywhere. Exciting, vibrant music has continued and does continue to happen unabated throughout the new millennium and into the 2010s. But the big difference is that most of the best music now really is going nowhere.

The number of new artists major labels release is decreasing year by year, and the things they do to minimise risks aren't always conducive to the overall health of the music scene. The music industry, including many independent labels and managers, has its own preferred way of promoting bands that can seem counterintuitive. A story I've heard more than once from musicians dealing with major labels is that the bands are discouraged from playing in their own venue circuit, where they could fill rooms with audiences who are genuinely into their music. Instead, they are pushed towards events that the label itself had approved – often in largely empty rooms to a handful of people we could politely describe as disinclined to pay them even the slightest attention. A big part of the idea behind this could well be to create scarcity, making each show matter more – many bands try to limit the number of shows they play for precisely this reason – but given the difference in the kind of crowd, there's more to it than that.

The Japanese music industry has a pathological need to control. It exerts near total control over most journalistic content, it tightly controls image rights, and it closely manages how individual bands interact with fans. By pushing bands into playing shows pre-approved by labels, perceptions of the band can be manipulated and they are often cleansed of the unwelcome taint of the dirty, unwashed live circuit. The band is placed in an environment where they are surrounded by professionals, and therefore cut off from their more anarchic immediate influences and the "wrong" kind of audience. Easing bands away from the scenes that nurtured them is close to standard practice, and also evidenced in the way major lab-els rebrand a new signing's first release for them as a "debut" even if the group has several releases on indie labels already behind them.

While the control of major labels isn't necessarily a bad thing for an individual band who wants to develop and become more professional, there is a damaging knock-on effect on the grassroots scene.

A typical scenario goes something like this: a scene starts to grow up around a few bands, a major label cherry picks the most promising one, that band then finds itself under more pressure to play the sort of gigs the label wants them it play, the scene loses its top band, and then, without the momentum that band was helping provide, the scene withers and dissipates. A diverse selection of bands plucked from here and there, then groomed for success by being surrounded by other professionally managed bands, creates a two-tier music scene with new ideas growing up from below before being cut off at the stem, with the ripest fruits plucked and added to a diverse but at the same time never really changing cauldron at the top.

Despite many challenges, there are two ways Japanese musicians can bypass the music industry's approved paths to success. The first and most difficult is for a scene or subculture to become so financially significant that it's impossible to ignore. This is what happened with otaku culture and the revival of idol music since the late 90s, and I'll be talking a lot about this later. The other way is to look abroad.

GOING OVERSEAS

It had seemed like such a good idea over drinks in the bar after the show. It had been one of those weekday gigs in Tokyo where it had become clear early on that no more than a handful of people were going to show up, but this had galvanised all the bands into making sure they gave it everything they could. The crowd had amped up the energy beyond what you'd have expected from its small size, and the bands had all supported each other – loudly and drunkenly. One of the bands was from the US, doing a self-booked DIY tour around Japan, and that had probably helped. The local acts wanted to leave them with a good impression of their time in Japan, and in the end it had been a special night: everyone was buzzing, and the touring Americans had struck up a particular friendship with one of the local bands.

"You should come to America! We can book you a few shows. Hell, we can go on tour together. Just leave it to us!"

"What do you think, guys? Shall we do it? Yeah, let's do it. Cheers!"

The email the guitarist had received from Cleveland a couple of months later had been a bit of a surprise to the Japanese band. Two weeks on the road around the Midwest and East Coast was a thrilling prospect. The problem was the bassist's job. And the singer's. And the drummer's family. Couldn't they just do five days? But then with flights for all four members coming in at $6,000 total, was it really worth it?

The guitarist had left it two weeks now without replying, and as he sat there staring at the email on his laptop screen for the hundredth time, he realised he was just looking for the right way to say no.

It is not easy for Japanese artists to tour overseas. A musician also working at a Japanese company gets about ten days off a year, which makes it impossible to do the sort of long tours necessary to recover expenses. Some musicians seek more flexible but low-paying jobs at warehouses or in care work. This way, they can work most of the year and save money for three-month European or American tours, but otherwise options are limited.

The difficulty of touring overseas affects the value artists place on their time, and a generation gap seems to have opened up between the Japanese groups who broke through abroad in the 90s and those ten years after.

"Kids these days are really organized," says Ichiro Agata from bubblegum-hardcore noise-punks Melt-Banana, "They want to do the record properly, planning the budget and everything. When they do a tour abroad, after just one tour maybe they'll see that it's unprofitable and find themselves asking if there's any point in doing it."

Similarly, Seagull Screaming Kiss Her Kiss Her's Aiha Higurashi pointed out in an interview that there has been a change in mindset among musicians.

"In the early 90s, Seagulls and Melt-Banana, we were the 'challenging' types," she explains, "[*Melt Banana vocalist Yako and I were*] female rock'n'rollers, going abroad and playing, releasing.

We were explorers. Recently, musicians are really wary."

While many of Melt-Banana's early overseas shows were basically played to empty rooms, younger bands tend to apply a much stricter cost-benefit analysis to their activities. Used to scrapping tooth and nail to make ends meet in the Japanese music scene's inverted business model, which treats musicians as customers of music-related services rather than workers, many bands simply can't justify the cost, and this again mitigates against regular and extensive overseas touring.

The difficulty of bands touring overseas and domestically may even be heightened by a gradual relaxing of Japanese social attitudes towards nonconformist lifestyles. As music has become less disgraceful an activity for decent members of society to engage in, more and more respectable people are making music: nice, middle class kids from good families pursuing creative hobbies while holding down full-time jobs. They have more to lose than the fiercely driven punk and underground weirdos who dropped out of society completely to blaze the trail in the 70s, 80s and early 90s that these new bands are now following. Also, thanks to the way the pay-to-participate contemporary Japanese indie scene allows any musician with a decent income to comfortably and easily play a couple of shows a month, they have way less to gain by throwing away their careers.

Another issue is that Japanese musicians tend to have a very Atlanticist view of music, equating "overseas" with the far away "West" and ignoring the rest of Asia for touring. Given the way the music press in Japan has tended to slavishly follow Anglophone (especially British) music journalists' notions of what's cool in an international context, this is perhaps not too surprising. When selecting sites for tours, there is also the perception – albeit one gradually losing hold – that the rest of Asia is somehow musically undeveloped or unsophisticated. On a more practical level, it is logistically challenging to tour Asia, while America and much of Europe exist as single markets with freedom of movement and a single currency. The cost of living in the West is generally comparable with Japan, whereas a vast discrepancy remains in between Japan and many of its neighbours, which mean that the fees bands can expect from Asian gigs have traditionally been next to worthless once translated into Japanese yen.

There are signs of this Western focus changing. Major talent agencies are pushing Japanese acts more aggressively in Asia, while promoters are bringing Chinese, Korean and Taiwanese acts to major Japanese festivals. The combination of growth among Southeast Asian economies and stagnation in Japan is also playing a role in putting touring between Japan and the rest of Asia more easily within reach. Nevertheless, the fact is that Japanese musicians tend to think of Europe and the United States as the centres of musical modernity, and when you look at global music this way, Japan is a backwater, far remote from the perceived London-New York axis of cool.

Distance shouldn't on its own act as an insurmountable barrier – Australia is even more isolated but its artists tour overseas. However, there are other factors in the mix that have deeper roots in Japanese culture. The first is obviously language, with every new generation wringing its hands about the parlous state of English education and warning of how Japan is falling behind the rest of the world due to people's lack of language skills. I don't know how true this really is, since my own experience is that there are plenty of musicians with decent enough English skills, and that in most cases a band who really wants to travel abroad can usually get by. Nevertheless, it's true that lack of confidence in language skills is widespread among Japanese people.

Together with anxiety over language, an ingrained sense of cultural difference makes some artists reluctant to tour overseas, and even defensive about how their music might be perceived abroad. There is a widespread idea, eagerly propagated by the Japanese media, that Japan is impossibly, incomprehensibly unique and strange to foreigners. News programmes rarely show reports about foreign events, and when they do, almost never in any real depth. TV programmes about foreign countries are usually filtered through the bug-eyed lens of a ditzy celebrity, emphasising how alien and weird it all is, and treating any points of commonality as jaw-droppingly wild and unexpected. Contact between Japanese and outsiders in the media is often portrayed as a novelty, and people internalise these infantile messages, even if they know in their heads that things aren't that simple.

Just as the Japanese media likes to portray the country as a mysterious land with four inscrutable seasons and perplexing eating implements, the Western media is happy to return the favour with its own Orientalising coverage that emphasises anything wacky, colourful and bizarre. Thus Japanese music is largely perceived in the West through a distorting lens, and the image of Japanese music I had growing up the UK was influenced greatly by this.

HOW JAPANESE MUSIC IS PERCEIVED ABROAD

It's a packed Thursday night at Moles club in Bath – a cosy venue once described by the NME as "a veal crate with a bar" – and a gang of Asian women take the stage. Dressed in a ragtag assortment of trashy glam-punk miniskirts and fishnets, they rip into a fuzzy, scuzzy, buzzsaw Buzzcocks riff and start singing.

"Better change your underpants / 'Cause you might need an ambulance / In the city!"

To the still teenage me in the audience, they're everything a Japanese band is supposed to be: rough, enthusiastic, cool and poppy, with a trashy, cartoonish punk aesthetic. "Contact Tokyo!" they scream out over the chorus, and I think to myself, "Yes! This is exactly what Tokyo must be like!"

The band is called Mika Bomb and they are from London.

Mika Bomb were my first contact with Japanese music, but they weren't really Japanese at all. The group's leader, Mika Handa, was an expat living in the UK, and while her band enjoyed playing with Japanese imagery, riffing off and subverting Western stereotypes of Asian femininity and other, broader cultural tropes, they were musically very much a product of the West. They played the *Purr* nights at Moles in Bath, which were tailor-made for their glam-punk aesthetic, and had links with gleefully trashy labels like Grand Royal and Damaged Goods. I loved them, but in the end I loved them the same way I loved bands like The Donnas and later Sahara Hotnights – their music was constructed entirely of elements that fell squarely within my existing frame of reference.

Later on, at university, a Japanese flatmate gave me a pile of cassettes of what was actually popular in Japan and I was knocked sideways. Globe, Mr. Children, Glay, SMAP, Miyuki Nakajima, Yumi Matsutoya, Eiichi Ohtaki – artists from the peak of the 90s J-Pop boom with a few "new music" legends thrown in. This music I had to work much harder to engage with. The sounds would occasionally remind me of something familiar – Mr. Children at this time retained new wave-ish echoes of Elvis Costello, while Globe had just enough techno and synthpop for me to parse it in some sort of familiar framework. Songs would start out with guitar riffs or beats that I recognised, and then the vocals would come in and the music would descend into something that felt like a childish nursery rhyme to me. Where were the blue notes? Why did the vocals have to stick so rigidly to the rhythm? Didn't they understand how this music was *supposed* to sound?

No, the Japanese music I liked was the wild stuff. The music on the crazy fringes. From Guitar Wolf's lo-fi garage rock junkheap to the robotic idol pop bubble gum perfection of Aya Matsuura, with almost nothing in between – that was the music I could connect to, and it took me a long, long time before I was able to grow accustomed to the sound of mainstream Japanese pop. Some mainstream pop, like SMAP, remains utterly loathsome to me. An important part of the reason I gravitated towards these extremes, however, was surely that by so definitively abandoning any sort of mainstream convention (acts from the Boredoms to Kyary Pamyu Pamyu are weird by Japanese as well as Western standards), they released me from the responsibility to connect on a level of familiarity. In order to gain a deeper understanding what was going on with Japanese pop, however, I needed to get inside the music and start to untangle what was going on under the hood.

There are musicological differences between Japanese and Anglo-American pop, even if the two traditions share a lot of conventions due to Western influences on all phases of Japanese music over the past century. While both Anglo-American and Japanese pop share very similar roots in jazz, Japan remains more influenced by classical melodic composition.

Japanese pop is also more likely to be tonal, rooted in a major or minor key, and employ more structural chord changes, whereas Anglo-American pop is more likely to be modal, not strictly major *or* minor, and to use chords more texturally.*

In terms of vocal melodies, there are differences rooted in language that have both rhythmical and melodic implications.

Japanese is what we might call a moraic language. Morae are

---

* I shan't claim to fully understand this, but essentially this seems to come down to the chord progression in tonal music known as the "dominant motion" which helps drive the song forward. In, say, the Dorian mode you can't really do that, so songwriters use ostinatos as a base around which to build the melodic tension.

similar to but distinct from syllables in that they include an element of time or "beats". For example, the word "Tokyo" has two syllables ("to-kyo") but four morae ("to-o-kyo-o" or more accurately "to-u-kyo-u"). Similarly, the "n" that ends the word "can" counts as one mora in its own right and gets a beat accordingly ("ca-n"). Another feature of Japanese is that each syllable or mora should have more or less equal stress.

This linguistic complication caused problems for early Japanese pop songwriters, because the Anglo-American pop traditions they were working within were designed around stress-timed English lyrics that were much more flexible in how words could contract or employ a melismatic effect, stretching syllables over multiple notes, or dropping in slightly before or after the beat to give the song a more conversational rhythm.

There are ways around this of course. *Enka* draws out nearly every syllable with exaggerated vibrato, while *yojohan* folk musicians employed a style called *hayakuchi kotoba* (literally "fast-mouth words", or maybe "tongue-twisters") where lyrics would be crammed at high speed into rhythmical spaces they clearly weren't designed to inhabit. Some 1970s "new music"-generation artists like Southern All Stars developed a vocal style that delivered Japanese words with an Anglicised inflection. Nevertheless, all these methods are highly stylised and not at all natural by the rhythmical standards of Japanese speech. They're also difficult, and it's worth noting that as karaoke became an increasingly important medium for the delivery of pop, the most popular songs would have increasingly needed to be ones that could be picked up and learned easily.

111

In any case, 1970s songwriters from Happy End onwards gradually developed a style of arranging vocals that worked around the features of the Japanese language rather than cramming the words into a rhythm that struggled to accommodate them. The melodies became increasingly moraic to fit the rhythm of Japanese language, and the relative flatness of Japanese intonation led to a convention where each syllable or mora was assigned its own pitch. As a result, to listeners brought up on a diet of Anglo-American pop, Japanese pop melodies vocal melodies can seem rigid and inflexible, married to the beat.

Which is not to say that Japanese pop is less sophisticated. In fact, one of the big differences between Japanese and Anglo-American pop is that if anything, Japanese pop is more musically sophisticated, employing far more complex patterns of chord changes than the traditional US/UK four-chord blues base allows for. Pop music everywhere is subject to its strictures and conventions, and anything you spend enough time immersed in can sound formulaic after a while.

So when Western listeners dismiss Japanese pop as being an inferior copy of its Western counterparts, what's often happening is that the listener is registering superficial, stylistic elements that he or she finds familiar, such as the synths or guitar playing style, but is being frustrated by melodies that, while hinting at something familiar, refuse to resolve themselves in the expected way.

Experimental and underground music from Japan is easier to export to dedicated listeners abroad than J-Pop. Since the 1960s, experimental musicians throughout the world have been exploring and incorporating sounds from wherever possible. Much of the Western interest in Japanese experimental music and noise in the 1990s came from an eagerness to dig up something different. Yet, the Japanese experimental bands that do well overseas tend still to be exotic within a familiar framework: Boris and Afrirampo's music often features blues-like chord progressions and Nisennenmondai employs familiar motorik and disco rhythms. Fans abroad still tend to gravitate towards what falls within their own systems of reference.

UK/US indie rock, while nominally independent and free-thinking, is in many ways locked even more than mainstream pop into a very Anglo-American songwriting tradition. In contrast, Japanese indie pop and rock tends to either look outward, adopting a position of slavish imitation of the "authentic" original, or focus inward, drawing from typical J-Pop chord progressions. Both these routes pose problems for Western listeners: Japanese imitations of Western acts offer nothing that can't be provided locally, while songs in the J-Pop tradition just sound wrong to ears not trained from an early age to find those chord progressions familiar.

In the 1990s, Shibuya-*kei* opened up one possible area for crossover. It emphasised, in addition to its love of 1980s British guitar pop, more experimental, Latin and jazz-based approaches that found sympathetic ears in the US alternative scene. In the other direction, the kind of progressive indie promoted by American labels like K Records shares common ground with elements of Japanese underground music (K has worked with Japanese artists like Maher Shalala Hash Baz, Moools, and

Tenniscoats). Overall though, while most reasonably popular British and American indie rock finds a willing audience and sympathetic press in Japan, Japanese rock bands of an equivalent status find it harder to make the reverse trip.

Japanophiles aside, the kind of Japanese music that tends to get attention overseas is the stuff that reinforces pre-existing notions of what Japan is like – particularly musicians whose imagery emphasise the exotic – but that at the same time doesn't challenge too strongly the prevailing Anglo-American-dominated mode of listening to music.

PROMOTING JAPANESE MUSIC ABROAD

"...And lastly, I want to thank Steve, the best organiser in the world!"

The crowd gives a roar of approval. They've heard of Steve. He's a legend, a whispered name, a fairy godmother. He's the guy who's been known to fly to Japan for the weekend just to see a gig by an indie band he's curious about. He's the mysterious Doctor Rock who every year plucks a handful of bands out of the Japanese indie underground and whisks them away to Canada for a short series of sold-out dates, all paid out of his surgical salary. He's the guy who just climbed up onstage and hurled himself into a crowd, borne aloft like some boreal Sun King on waves of good vibes, buoyed by his own irrepressible enthusiasm.

The punkish young alt-rock band onstage is called Pens+ and they have just returned from one of Steve's tours. Right now, they and the other bands from the tour are holding a swinging, celebratory coda to the tour – an opportunity for them and their home crowd to say thanks to their magical benefactor.

Canada: The promised land.

The biggest problem with introducing Japanese music overseas is the notion of "Japanese music" in the first place. Once labelled as such, it forces analysis of the work through the prism of its nationality and compounds the difficulty it is already likely to face in trying to find an appropriate musical niche. Nevertheless, the Japanese music/culture package arrangement is still many people's preferred mode of delivering bands from Japan to overseas audiences.

Given that one of the government's prime motivations in its stumbling efforts to support Japanese pop culture abroad is the promotion of Japanese "soft power", it's natural that state-sponsored initiatives tend to emphasise the music's nationality over its genre or style. One of the most heavily publicised of such initiatives has been the "Cool Japan" fund, ridiculed by the artist Takashi Murakami in an interview with the Asahi newspaper as narcissistic and, "Little more than a catchphrase for advertisers trying to get public money." Certainly some of the most visible manifestations of initiatives like Cool Japan has been the process whereby idol groups are sent off to play culture expos abroad, whereupon shills on Japanese TV variety shows breathlessly inform audiences that such-and-such a band is now popular with foreigners. Such Potemkin Village-style events play well with the media back in Japan, but they are meaningless abroad.

Another problem with Cool Japan is that it is an initiative of the Ministry of Economy, Trade and Industry, not the Ministry of Culture. This means that the money it has is treated like venture capital, not cultural infrastructure. With cuisine that might be a valid approach, but when the state starts looking for visible returns on its investment in art, you lose all the great exploratory and experimental work that brings no specific

116

financial benefit but which lays the groundwork for other, perhaps more commercially-minded artists to build on. Japanese music is at precisely that "groundwork" level in terms of its penetration in the West, with most artists being unfamiliar, and the music based on a songwriting tradition that has diverged in some key ways from Western styles.

Cool Japan is essentially a top-down initiative that's purpose is using the country's culture as a vehicle for promoting Japan's brand. For individual promoters, however, the motivations and goals are going to be slightly different, even if they sometimes use a similar approach, focusing on the music's nationality and exoticism. Another poorly thought out attempt to appeal to foreign music listeners was Tofu Records. Set up as a US outlet for Sony Music Entertainment Japan, it aimed to use the anime community as a base from which to introduce Japanese music into the United States. It fell into a similarly fallacious line of thinking as Cool Japan: anime is cool → anime is Japanese → J-Pop is Japanese → J-Pop must also be cool. Sony compounded the error by starting out late in 2003, at a time when anime's edgy 90s appeal had mostly passed in the West and the medium was starting to take on a more infantile aspect. Put simply: in mid-2000s America, if you went around saying you were into J-Pop, people would think you were creepy and possibly a paedophile.

Now that's not to say anime and J-Pop don't have a market in the West – evidently they do. Rather it means that the market they have is of a very different nature to the Japanese domestic equivalent, and the kind of business practices that work in the latter will not always meet with the same success in the former.

The truth is that Cool Japan has so far been primarily for Japanese domestic consumption, using a carefully stage-managed version of the rest of the world as a mirror to assuage Japanese cultural anxiety. It is often driven by advertising agencies, management offices and major labels, whose main goal is to promote their own clients or contracted stars, which gives it an inevitable bias towards the existing J-Pop mainstream. In the pop music world, the result has therefore typically been unadventurous, focusing on art and culture that is already popular in Japan and delivering it in a familiar, unimaginative way to markets that have little scope for expansion in their current form.

As an integral part of the mainstream, major labels like Tofu's parent company Sony exert top-down control over what gets popular through their marketing departments, treating DIY music scenes (with their structure of building from the ground up) as simply convenient spawning grounds from which labels can pluck new talent to be fed into the machine. Substance and identity are not part of the major label modus operandi, and they don't need to be, as long as those spawning grounds are still healthily producing new talent. In the American market, Sony Music Entertainment Japan has no full-spectrum media penetration and anime fans are too culturally isolated a group to be a substitute for a core music audience from which the music can grow outward. Indie labels and promoters, on the other hand, tend to organise from the ground up, and as a result are often institutionally better suited to building bridges overseas.

On a smaller scale to some of these government- and major-led efforts – but with more successful results – has been the Japan Nite event and tour that Audrey Kimura of the Benten label organises in conjunction with South By Southwest (SXSW).

Benten is a small indie label – two really, as it includes the Sister Records companion label – started in the mid-90s with a roster predominantly composed of female musicians playing colourful, slightly batty, lo-fi garage-punk, and it was this image that cemented the label's identity as well as that of the early US tours. Benten marketed themselves, like Sony's Tofu Records, on their Japaneseness, but perhaps recognising a preconception among American audiences of Japanese music as being wacky and off-the-wall, their booking policy had a bit more spice and fun to it than the J-Pop mainstream. However, Benten were also rooted in a distinctive musical identity. The Japanese focus in this case is a matter of practicality – if you're booking bands from Japan, *of course* it's going to be a "Japan bands tour" – and it's an obvious and handy marketing hook. The image of colourful silliness is perhaps more a happy coincidence, since Benten's roster was already biased towards wacky, off-the-wall artists prior to any overseas adventures. Nevertheless, it was useful in marketing the tours, since it promised the combination of exoticism and reinforcement of preconceptions that ensures audiences can easily grasp at a moment's notice the kind of thing they're going to get. The fact Sister/Benten had an identifiable garage-punk centred musical identity provided what Tofu Records so catastrophically failed to: give the actual product substance.

So Benten and their Japan Nite tours built an audience from the ground up by having a recognisable, coherent product to sell, and through sheer persistence, going back year after year after year. Now whether that approach is scaleable to the level that Sony/Tofu were aiming for it's hard to say, but the work Japan Nite has done building a reputation and a "brand" has at least paid off in its own small way, and allowed Kimura & co. the freedom to gradually row back on the wacky Japanese stereotypes, expanding their booking policy to cover all manner of Japanese pop and rock that they deem interesting.

That's not to say Japan Nite is an unqualified success story at promoting Japanese bands abroad. It relies on sizeable up-front costs from the artists themselves that are then partially recouped by the short tour. Some bands also balk at the emphasis on Japan and Japaneseness in how it is composed and marketed – a view particularly strong in those indie bands with the most internationally-focused sets of influences. While it's easy to see these bands as snobbish and elitist, preferring to see themselves as part of a global indie community and viewing any emphasis on their Japaneseness as hopelessly parochial, the success of Japanese music abroad in the long run will depend on it being accepted as just music rather than as "Japanese music". Japan Nite by its very nature isn't there yet, but in a world where success stories for Japanese music abroad are few and far between, it's important to acknowledge the lessons its model offers.

Another Japanese band package tour that follows a similar model is Steven Tanaka's *Next Music From Tokyo* Canadian event, which focuses on more technical post-rock and prog-pop acts, the costs of which, despite capacity crowds in the hundreds, Tanaka has generally underwritten at massive financial cost to himself.

In Tanaka's case, his aim was more to recreate some of the atmosphere and sense of community he felt going to indie events in Japan, with the Tokyo Boredom underground events and festivals a key influence.

"My ideal audience would be open-minded indie fans," says Tanaka, "The sort of audience you might call 'Japanophiles' are welcome, but they're not the core of what I'm aiming the event at. The most important thing though is that I don't want to perpetuate the 'weird Japan' stereotype."

With this set of intentions in mind, one of Tanaka's big successes has been not only in finding an audience for Japanese indie music in Canada, but also in recreating some of the Japanese scene's DIY spirit, his own enthusiasm buoying along others who have helped him promote and grow the event.

Obviously there are limits to how far an event based on that kind of independent, communal spirit can grow, and without becoming much bigger, the economic model would be unsustainable for most people. Baltimore promoter and musician Michael Young has been bringing more caustic postpunk-orientated bands over for short tours of the U.S. East Coast but again, something has to give financially, in this case from the bands' side.

Like Tanaka, Young is keen that the bands be understood on their own virtues explaining that, "The crowd I would aim for would definitely be gathering based on the performer, either from how big they are, to what their sound is, and how they are as people."

Nevertheless, he again has to recognise that the Japaneseness – the promise of something different – is part of the band's appeal. Speaking to Melt-Banana back in 2013, guitarist Ichiro Agata suggested that the general level of interest American audiences have in Japanese music seems to have declined from the pioneering days of the 90s, Michael Young believes it still carries a boost in the local live circuit though.

"Many people in the USA still get excited when foreign bands or performers come," he states, "So gathering a crowd is pretty easy for an underground performer."

Rather different to Tanaka and Young's approaches, Tom Smith of London-based JPU Records' work with the Japan Underground event reveals some important points pertaining to how Japanese music is received abroad.

Superficially similar in many ways to the Sony/Tofu approach, Smith tends to work with more mainstream Japanese acts, including idols, visual-*kei* bands and straightforward J-pop acts, but JPU Records' approach highlights three key divisions, that, while fundamental features of the Japanese music scene when it's at home, simply cease to exist in the same way as soon as the music goes abroad.

Firstly, the divisions between genres that exist in Japan, separating the mods from the punks, the indie kids from the technopop tribe, the singer-songwriters from the electronic knob-twitchers, are eliminated overseas – partly due to different alignments of genre divisions and partly by how the music's very Japaneseness can overwhelm perception of its genre.

"My experience in Japan is the audiences are quite segregated," says Smith, "I've had Japanese people tell me that they wish Japan Underground existed in Japan. They tell me that in Japan, fans that like visual-*kei* will often JUST like visual-*kei* and ignore other kinds of music. Or they'll like just a certain type of indie rock sound. But at Japan Underground, the audience and the music played is a real mixture that wouldn't really work well in Japan."

The second division is the one between domestic and overseas music. In Japan, foreign and domestic music are treated as entirely separate things, with record stores sometimes segregating them onto completely different floors. In the UK, on the other hand, foreign music as a distinct market category doesn't exist in such a clearly defined and independent way. This means that a UK-based promoter with some understanding of both the Japanese and British music landscapes can sometimes see connections between a Japanese artist and a potential UK audience that a Japanese company operating in a market with strict domestic/foreign segregation wouldn't necessarily. Discussing his own work with JPU Records and the Japan Underground events, Smith cites the appeal of visual-*kei*/metal band The GazettE to nu-metal fans and alt-rock band Ling Tosite Sigure to indie/shoegaze fans as examples of how these crossovers can occur.

Lastly, the division between underground and mainstream becomes distorted once a band leaves Japan's shores, and this can complicate things for those promoting Japanese music overseas. While Smith admits that as he has signed and promoted more major acts from Japan he sometimes regrets the "Japan Underground" event name, the fact is that even the most mainstream Japanese music is still consumed in an underground fashion by UK audiences.

"I get the snooty indie kids on Twitter poking fun at the 'underground' part of the name and the event not really focusing on 'underground' artists from Japan," explains Smith, "I mean, I'll DJ tracks from X Japan, Radwimps, Maximum the Hormone, etc. They're right: it isn't underground at all. But at the same time, I don't believe that's necessarily true. Yes, they might be major bands in Japan, but here it's still very underground. You won't read about the bands in magazines or newspapers, you won't hear them on the radio, you won't see them on TV. You'll probably only find out about them because you have one friend that talks about them non-stop and will share a link with you or let you borrow an album. To me, that's the 'underground' element."

Of course, the way the internet works means that major acts with expensive promotional videos and a strong position in Japanese media, both regular and social, will still tend to have an advantage both domestically and internationally over genuinely underground Japanese acts. However, major label embargos on online content and even press samples of new albums can be a major hurdle for those like Smith trying to promote them overseas.

Even overseas promoters and labels who deal with relatively

mainstream Japanese acts operate on very fine profit margins or outright losses, and the more Japanese bands there are on the tour, the bigger and more likely the financial losses become. The indie bands who make money on U.S. or European tours are those who devote months at a time to constant touring and gigging, playing alongside like-minded local bands with the support of like-minded local promoters. Over the past couple of decades, a lengthy tour model has worked best for bands like Melt-Banana, Acid Mothers Temple and Ultra Bide, who have arranged their whole lives around music.

However, most of those bands also benefitted from Japanese music's newness and exoticism to 1990s and early 2000s audiences. While this exotic appeal still exists to a certain extent, there's only a certain degree to which a promoter can say, "Hey, look! Japanese!" and expect people to care before they start to say, "Oh, *another* oddball Japanese experimental punk band – whatevs!" The sense of novelty that accompanied the noise boom of the early 90s and the later international crossover of Shibuya-*kei* has faded, and the increasingly easy access to Japanese music online has lessened the wow factor. In this sense, the perception of Japanese music abroad as just "music" rather than something exotic and wacky is double-edged: for something that's *just music* like all the local bands that are already clamouring for attention, Japanese acts are extraordinarily expensive and difficult to promote. Once you remove the Japaneseness as a selling factor, how do you sell a band and why should someone go to see them over any other band?

Ideally, all music fans and promoters would recognise

Japanese music's nuances and a connection could be forged between bands and overseas audiences without presenting touring acts as alien cultural artefacts. While the combination of familiar sounds with an unfamiliar musical approach can make Japanese artists disconcerting and alienating, it can also work in their favour if presented in the right way. A big part of the appeal of Japanese music is, as JPU Records' Tom Smith suggests, how bands take a familiar influence and, "somehow adapt it to sound similar, but new."

Supporting local promoters who are already trying to find ways of connecting Japanese music to overseas audiences is where government funding could help in more productive ways than sending idols to dance around on stages at Parisian expos. If the government wants to help, it should establish an independent body that can support cooperation between Japanese and overseas artists, promoters and audiences; provide financial support to help overcome some of the obstacles caused by Japan's geographical remoteness; and maybe also use the funds to ease some artists, organisers or promoters through the difficult early days before making the breakthrough they need to be able to support themselves. Focusing on grassroots operators and international cooperation may not provide the flashy video presentations that look a bit like "results" if you squint enough; however, it's a far better way of getting artists to audiences primed to appreciate them on their musical virtues. In my interviews with both Tanaka and Young they made a point of stressing the technical skill and showmanship of Japanese bands as particular strengths they see as common, but the sort of music they promote is far distant from the image government-related projects have typically sought to project. Even Smith and JPU Records, who have promoted more mainstream acts that fit more comfortably into the wild and colourful image of Japanese pop culture, have had to do so by introducing them in a way that connects them with the existing realities of British music fandom. If the "brand" of Japanese music abroad absolutely must be promoted in a top-down manner (and I'm not convinced of this) by government-sponsored agencies, it's important that those tasked with doing so don't end up pandering to reductive stereotypes like "wierd Japan" and overemphasising niches like anime or Harajuku fashion. Rather it should emphasise quality and diversity, promoting an image of Japanese culture flexible enough that individual promoters can connect Japan's music with local scenes in whatever way makes the best fit – be that anime music, idol groups, post-rock, noise, indiepop, metal, electro-house or any number of utterly unclassifiable things.

NEITHER LOVE NOR MONEY – THE LIVE HOUSE

I'm at a show in Tokyo: there are maybe seven or eight people scattered around the venue, clinging to the shadows of UFO Club's dark red and black gloom like off-duty ghouls in an after-hours dive bar in Hell.

"We are all prostitutes," announces a girl's voice, "Everyone has their price."

In a trembling cadence she recites The Pop Group's words in Japanese translation, then the shrill drone of a cheap synthesiser cuts through the air as the bass and drums clatter and clang their way through a propulsive, lo-fi Krautrock instrumental. It sends a familiar chill through the spine, but today something feels wrong.

Bum notes start to creep in as the set progresses. The guitarist starts casting sharp glances over at the bassist. She glowers back at him. The personal drama unfolding onstage seems to be informing the more abstract drama of the music as it rises to an emotional crescendo.

"If I die, will the world freeze?

Or will it vanish in the eastern sky,

Just like nothing happened?"

The girl collapses to her knees, buries her face in her hands and starts sobbing. She remains there, motionless but for the occasional gasp or shudder, for the remainder of the set as the other two members finish awkwardly around her. The curtains close on the stage to a polite smattering of disinterested applause.

In the entrance hall upstairs, the guitarist approaches me with a huge grin plastered across his face.

"Best gig ever!"

For most musicians in Japan, it's in the domestic live circuit that they find themselves trying to grind out gigs and get noticed, and this can be a dispiriting experience.

As an audience member, going to gigs in Japan is one of the least efficient ways of discovering good music, which is probably why so few people do it. Even if you take my approach of finding one band you like and stalking them ruthlessly, you'll still find yourself sitting through hours of the most dire, self-regarding, yowling, whining dross before you find that one other band you like. And, at around 2000 yen or more for most tickets, plus the customary 500 yen compulsory drink charge, it's easy to understand why so few people think live music is worthwhile in Japan.

Finding good stuff in music venues requires time and money. In an era where most bands have a Soundcloud or Bandcamp page, or at least the ghost of a Myspace that they haven't updated in five years, there are other, easier ways of finding music for the lazy music fan. The trouble is that music that sounds great through your laptop's speakers at 2 AM isn't necessarily going to be the same music that sounds good raging out of a PA stack from three feet away. Some music you really do need to see live, but gaining initial access to it can be frustrating.

A big part of the problem is the sheer amount of music there is. Let's say there are about 500 live venues in the extended Tokyo area. I have no idea if that's an accurate figure, as there are clubs, bars and studios all over town that have live music some nights but not others, but in Koenji there are about 15 live venues, with a similar number in Shinjuku, more in Shimo-Kitazawa and even more in Shibuya. Pretty much every stop along the Chuo and Sobu Lines has a handful, and there are more scattered throughout the city. 500 sounds to me like a reasonable average of estimates.

Now multiply that figure by an average of four bands a night. That's 2,000 bands playing every night in Tokyo. Then multiply by 30 and that's 60,000 over the course of a month. OK, a few of those are going to be the same bands playing twice and not all these venues, especially the more rural ones, are going to be open every night, but even so, we're looking at a massive amount of live music going on pretty much constantly. Now think about how many of those acts are going to be any good. The correct answer is, "As close to zero as statistically makes no difference."

So assume you have somehow managed to find half a dozen decent bands out of this seething mass of mediocrity and downright dismalness, how can you guarantee seeing them all in one place? The answer to that one is either give up or book your own damn event.

I chose the second option.

But how does one go about booking a live event? There are *lots* of venues to choose from in Tokyo, and the costs of renting one vary from nothing to hundreds of thousands of yen. On average, an audience of 50 or 60 people will cover the cost of renting the space for an event, which might not seem like much for a lineup of five bands, but the crowd at a typical weekday night show will rarely be more than a third of that, often much less. Even on weekends, a full house is far from guaranteed. This is why for most of their own band bookings most Tokyo venues have since the mid-80s band boom adopted a system called *noruma* – derived, hopefully with some irony, from the Russian word for production quotas in the gulags, but connoting what would be called "pay-to-play" in English – in which bands are given a quota of tickets to sell. Usually bands need to unload between 10 and 25 tickets, before they see any money, and for anything below that quota the bands have to pay the venue. When you go to a gig in Japan and the guy at the door asks you who you're there to see, that's why they do it: they're marking you off the fee the band's going to have to pay the venue at the end of the night.

Everyone hates *noruma*. It is the single most universally despised thing in the entire music scene. Bands hate paying it, booking staff at venues hate asking bands to pay it, and audiences don't understand it. *Noruma* sucks.

At its worst it's an outright scam, with booking staff for venues basically cast in the role of telemarketers, scanning the web for young bands, flattering them with the promise of a doorway to fame and recognition and then hitting them with the fee. Another popular move is the compilation album curated by the venue, which the featured bands pay for themselves and which no one ever buys. It should be noted, however, that rare exceptions like UFO Club's rather good compilation series do exist.

Even the best venues, staffed by well-connected musicians with a deep knowledge of the scene, usually support a small number of their favourite artists on the back of bands paying to play to near empty rooms. In this scenario, the bands paying *noruma* do time on the weekday dead shifts, and in exchange get connections and the chance to play with what we might call the "senior" bands, with the possibility of eventually moving up to the elite rung themselves, where they will be afforded the hallowed status of being able to play gigs on weekends for no pay.

The basic problem is that property is expensive in Tokyo, and ticket prices and drink sales simply don't bring in enough money by themselves to keep venues open. Live venues must reconcile the enormous financial burden placed on them by Tokyo land prices with the fact that they occupy a status and level of respectability comparable with, if not a little lower than, the sex industry.

No one wants a live venue near their homes or businesses, which is one of the reasons clubs tend to cluster around shady parts of town, near hostess bars, brothels and love hotels. Noise is part of this, although most venues are soundproofed to such a degree that you'd have to be a borderline unstable, obsessive-compulsive control freak to have a problem with it. More important than noise is the way Japan takes the fear most countries have of young people standing in the streets, doing nothing, and magnifies it to pathological extremes. In a culture where any activity that isn't either working or spending money is something best done in the privacy of one's own home, loitering is an act of shameless disgrace. What if children were to see? What kind of example would it set them? What if other business' customers were to see? They might feel *uncomfortable*!

In fact, even the sex industry establishments seem to view live venues only with the most grudging tolerance, putting the management under pressure to ensure lowlife music fans don't congregate on the street outside and put off their more respectable and lucrative clientele. So public tolerance of live rock music and clubs is always on a hair trigger, with the result that where venues do operate, they do so with the very strict understanding that they keep themselves as low-key as possible. Any noise complaints from neighbours or problems local businesses have with scruffy youngsters loitering outside bring swift retribution from the police – or polite visits from the local gangsters, depending on the nature of the complainant's business. This forces many venues to finish all live music around 10:00pm, while until recently the same sex industry laws that regulate the music scene banned dancing after 1:00am in most other establishments. Coupled with the working hours of many Japanese, who are often in offices past 8:00pm, and a lack of late-night transport services, many are excluded from attending concerts even if they want to. The result is that venues find themselves on an economic as well as a legal knife-edge. There are some solutions that have been proposed to solve this problem, but none of them offer complete solutions to the economic, social and legal problems live music faces.

(1) Make tickets cheaper and more people will come

This is certainly true up to a point. Ticket prices in Tokyo and throughout Japan are stupidly expensive: easily double the equivalent prices in London and quadruple what you could expect to pay in somewhere like LA. Making prices cheaper does encourage more people to come, but not enough. Events in rehearsal studios and some other kinds of music bars, where they've compromised on the number of staff employed and/or the quality of the sound gear, are often half price compared to normal live venues in Tokyo, but halving the ticket price doesn't bring in double the audience. Of course a larger audience buys more drinks, and if venues were willing to loosen their grip on the bar money, formalising a system where event organisers receive a portion of the drink profits over a certain quota could encourage more events to take risks with lower ticket prices. Some venues will make allowances or give bonuses when drink sales are high, but rarely on anything other than an ad hoc basis. Given the low and declining alcohol consumption generally among young people in Japan, one must have at least some sympathy with the venues' caution here.

(2) Make drinks cheaper and you'll sell more off the bar

Probably true up to a point, but again not by enough. I've known several venues that have tried setting a ¥300 instead of ¥500 standard drinks price and almost without exception they were forced to put the prices up after a while. The truth is that young people in Japan are drinking less and less every year. One venue manager I spoke to complained bitterly about an event with a capacity crowd of a hundred people, and when it came time to tot up drink sales at the end of the night, they'd sold one single drink over the minimum compulsory order the audience pays for upon entry. The hard drinking music fan is a dying species in modern Japan.

(3) Make the venues nicer and they'll be more attractive places to hang out at

Live venues in Tokyo tend to be drab, featureless places, with rare exceptions – the gorgeous Aoi Heya in Shibuya for example. A typical venue will simply be a black oblong with a bar at one end and a stage at the other: functionality incarnate but a place designed for standing in darkness, staring at a band, not for socialising or having any other kind of fun. One possible reason for this is that venues are seen as interchangeable spaces while the best events and organisers move around from one place to another, bringing their own atmosphere with them wherever they pitch camp. Giving the venue itself too much character might limit moneymaking opportunities from different kinds of event. That aside, it's hard to argue with the suggestion that the best venues in Tokyo tend to be the ones with a bit of personality, either in their interior design and layout, or their provision of food or seated areas depending on the type of music they encourage – which brings us onto this next and perhaps most important point.

(4) Have a coherent booking policy

Rather than just taking the money from any band who's willing to pay them, if venues could provide some semblance of coherence in the sort of music they put on, either through focusing on a specific type of music or by having clearly defined nights devoted to certain styles, it would be much easier for audiences to know what to expect. One idea from the West that could perhaps be imported might be that of band residencies, where a slow Monday or Tuesday night is given over to one band or organiser for a month, who then books their own support acts and at the end of the month, if it goes well, maybe gets a bit of money. This residency system would reinforce the identity of the venue and help forge relationships with bands, perhaps making the venue more attractive to other artists who might hope to get their own residencies in the future. There are problems of course, first among which is the perennial one of whether the venue could expect to recover the same money from the residency nights that they would from renting the stage to bands. A second problem is that since most musicians are juggling their bands with often restrictive work and family lives, finding people able to do four successive Tuesdays would likely be difficult.

One thing that links these ideas to make venues more sustainable is that the strategies are all predicated on the notion of the audience as the consumer. In a standard economic model, the situation with live music in Tokyo is clearly an excess of supply and grossly insufficient demand, so the natural response should be for a large number of venues to close down and keep doing so until the supply starts to match the demand again.

Instead, what has happened is that venues recognise that amateur bands are willing to pay a certain amount for the privilege of performing on a stage – of playing at being a rock band for a night – and in that realisation, the artist themselves becomes the consumer and the audience is cut out of the equation: "Hey, audience! You're poor, you don't drink enough and you have dismal taste in music, we don't need you anymore!"

Now this sounds bad, but it might not be all bad. For one thing, it means that bands have access to high quality amps, drum kits and PA systems that they would otherwise have to buy or rent themselves and then lug around to gigs. More significantly perhaps, it also affects the kind of music that gets played.

Given how unmitigatedly awful basically all popular music in Japan is, finding fans for something imaginative and offbeat takes time, and what *noruma* does, as long as the bands can scrape together the money, is allows them to do whatever they damn well like onstage for half an hour with top quality sound equipment. Usually that's something utterly dreary and self-obsessed, or perhaps something offensively masturbatory, but at least it doesn't always sound like Sekai no Owari.

And sometimes the alternative scene is really marvellous. The best local shows in Tokyo are composed almost entirely of bands who, were it left to audience numbers alone, would never get gigs. As it is, however, bands making uncommercial, often dizzyingly fresh, avant-garde or just plain weird postpunk, are a sizeable presence at several venues to the point where they could legitimately be called a scene.

Now I'm not saying *noruma* has caused scenes to coalesce, but it certainly made it easier to get those bands together initially. How you progress from there is the challenge. As Number Girl's Kentaro Nakao succinctly explained to me, "Nowadays for musicians it's easier to get started, but much harder to keep going."

For bands and venues to be sustainable in the long-term, concerts must be booked in a way that brings in enough people to ensure no one loses money. In a city like Tokyo, where almost no good music is popular and hardly any popular music is good, being able to negotiate niche subscenes is essential.

NEGOTIATING SCENE POLITICS

The gig is over, but another little performance is just beginning. The venue staff are pulling out tables and chairs, and preparing snacks. The organiser is frantically trying to sort the lingering audience and band members into those who will stay for a drink and those who will go, collecting money from the former and distributing thanks and well wishes to the latter.

Two young guys from the audience wait patiently to talk to one of the musicians. He's busy holding court with a group of friends from one of the other bands. He's just released an album and his video is getting some airplay on Space Shower TV. He's a little more famous than his friends now, but they're older than him so he remains polite. His friends have to get their last train home, because they're recording their own album the next day. They make a point of casually mentioning the engineer, who is both older and more famous than Mr. Space Shower.

Seeing a chance, the two young guys approach him and congratulate him on his band's set. They say they're friends of his bass player, which is partly true – the bass player is everyone's friend when he's drunk. They have a band too: they're members of the same live music club at university that the musician used to belong to, and his band are a big inspiration to them. They'd be really honoured if he could play an event that they're organising.

The musician accepts their praise with the indulgent air of one merely receiving the tribute to which he is entitled, but when the topic of the event comes up he cuts them short.

"Listen," he says, "It simply wouldn't be appropriate for us to play with you at this stage. You're just not at the level yet where you can make an invitation like that to us."

The two young guys nod along, humbly realising they've made a faux pas. In their starry-eyed ambition they have overextended themselves – reached too far above their station. Of course at this stage in the musician's career it would be wrong for him to be seen sharing a stage with these newcomers – especially in the context where they are organisers and he a guest. Perhaps if they work the scene for a while, deal with some bands closer to their own status for a while, they might get the chance to open for a bill with them sometime in the future. Before that happens, however, they need to know their place.

The organiser cuts in at this point and asks the young guys if they are staying for the after-party. They arrange their faces into smiles of gratitude and hand over the money. There are still a lot of other people in the room, and they're going to have their work cut out for them building connections.

When you're putting together an event in Tokyo, there are a lot of factors beyond simple economics that you need to take into account.

Personally, I've nearly always put on my events in Tokyo's neighbourhood of Koenji because that's where I live and I'm lazy: if a venue is more than ten minutes' walk from my flat, it's too far. It's also a good place because the town itself is lovely, and little things like the walk from the station to the venue have a subtle, positive influence on audience members' moods before they enter. The fact that Koenji is a bit out of the way from the big commercial hubs on the Yamanote train line means that the neighbourhood has a more local atmosphere to it as well, a sense of identity as a place not just where music happens but also where it lives. A lot of the people who go to gigs in Koenji are also people who live there, which adds a sense of intimacy that you don't get so often in more centrally located venues.

Other factors a budding organiser might consider include: Are the staff friendly? Is the venue well known among fans of the kinds of bands you're planning on booking? What are the drink prices like? What do the toilets smell like and are they positioned conveniently?* For bands trying to organise their own events, they also have to consider their social position in the music scene's hierarchy.

Musician and music journalist Ryotaro Aoki grew up in the US but cut his teeth as a musician after returning to Japan, where he felt the wild and uninhibited face that Japanese underground music shows to the world often conceals a surprisingly conservative social undercurrent.

"There's a way you're supposed to operate as an indie or alternative band that was established in the Number Girl/Quruli days, around and just after 2000," Aoki says, "You play at venues,

---

* The position of bathrooms in selecting a venue may not seem that important, but the toilet at Koenji Muryokumuzenji is actually behind the stage, which means that audience members either have to shove past the performing band or run to the nearest convenience store for an emergency mid-set wee. As far as smell is concerned, the toilets at the otherwise very nice venue Jam in Shinjuku are notorious, to the point where it's almost a badge of pride.

pay *noruma*, go to *uchiage* [after-party or post-gig drinking session], get to know bands. Very formulaic."

This process of networking, or as Aoki puts it "dick-sucking", goes hand in hand with a social dynamic based on whether one is a *sempai* (senior) or *kohai* (junior) in the hierarchy. A *kohai* band needs to pay their respects and dues at all the intervening rungs of the ladder before they can invite certain *sempai* to perform at one of their events.

"These mainstream Japanese social values that you'd have thought the underground scene wouldn't need or care about," continues Aoki, "You'd think people would be more open-minded and could get past that."

Not everyone subscribes to this hierarchical system though. The "Hakata no wave" scene that gathered around bands like Number Girl and Panicsmile was partly a reaction against the closed, hierarchical culture that had built up around Fukuoka's older "*mentai* rock" scene. Other bands just don't play the game and manage to find a way through on their own.

"There are two types of bands," explains Ichiro Agata of Melt-Banana, "There are bands who do events and create a community and try hard that way, and then there are bands like us who will come and play if you invite us, but we're not going to go out of our way and send gifts so someone will ask us to play."

A big problem that I encountered when beginning to book my own events in Tokyo was that for even the tiniest sliver of hope that people were going to show up, all the bands had to sound exactly the same. Absolutely everyone would *tell* me they liked diversity, but I soon realised it was box office poison:

people would actively flee it.

This segregation is perhaps partly behind the reason foreigners in Tokyo find it so hard to navigate their way through the music scene. For someone like Aoki, growing up in the States and initially experiencing Japanese music from a foreigner's perspective, the bands from Japan who gain recognition overseas simply didn't provide him with the tools needed to start finding his way through all the city's musical cul de sacs.

"Bands like Melt-Banana, Boris," explains Aoki, "all these bands I found in high school in the States I had no context for, just that people were talking about them on message boards. I pictured this diverse scene where all these bands existed, but then actually being here and seeing them, and talking to them, I understood that they left here because they didn't fit in."

In smaller Japanese cities than Tokyo, fewer venues means that bands and audiences are more used to rubbing up against music from different genres. The capital's scenes, on the other hand, tend to be fragmented into factionalised niches – sometimes even among seemingly similar sounding bands. Ad hoc groups generally form and disperse seemingly at random around groups of musicians who make friends with each other, around venues with sympathetic booking policies, and around little DIY fashion movements. Often these scenes are subdivided on territorial grounds, and two oddly separated crowds that I frequently encounter in my booking activities are ones which I'm going to loosely summarise here as Chuo Line bands and Setagaya bands.

Musically there's not much difference between these two

subscenes, with musicians from both worlds likely to have some background influence coming from postpunk and no wave, 80s UK indie rock, maybe Krautrock, and probably American 90s alt rock as well. Basically a set of influences you would largely expect to be mutually compatible. They also share a more or less DIY ethos and tend to self-release their own music. The difference is a subtler one and falls more along social and even philosophical lines.

Setagaya bands

- Parties organised by scenesters and DJ teams
- Tend to use the cheapest and easiest venues
- Events usually around or near Shibuya or Shimo-Kitazawa
- More likely to speak (and sing in) English
- More likely to have connections with and be influenced by contemporary overseas bands
- Make fanzines
- No tote bags
- No website but active on Tumblr and Bandcamp
- Avoid paying *noruma*
- More fashionable, younger fans
- Sell own tote bags

- Parties organised by venues or bands
- Use venues with sympathetic booking policies and good sound
- Events tend to be along the Chuo Line between Kichijoji and Shinjuku
- Less likely to speak (and sing in) English
- Less well connected with overseas music scenes and more likely to be influenced by local peers and Japanese underground/alternative tradition
- HTML web site and possibly still on Myspace (although the latter had mostly died out by the time of writing)
- Did time paying *noruma* for sparsely attended weekday gigs
- Unfashionable, older fans

Now from these dreadful and unfair generalisations, a couple of themes emerge: Setagaya bands are more internationally-minded, more web-savvy, sharper when it comes to exploiting merchandise opportunities, and see music as part of a wider lifestyle package. Chuo Line bands are more locally focused, tend to be slower in adapting to the web, seeing it as more an annoyance than an opportunity, and focus on music to the exclusion of pretty much anything else.

None of these characteristics are uniquely Japanese, but there is something particular to Tokyo about how strict it is. Go to almost any other city in Japan and the scene is too small for this to be an issue; however, the hyper-fragmentalisation of the Tokyo indie scene reveals this fault line even among artists making loosely similar music. Admittedly these are dangerously loaded terms, but we can perhaps summarise them as inward- and outward-looking tendencies. In this way, the current Japanese music scene is roughly divided between these two world views: thus, a band like Melt-Banana, whose musical hinterland lies more among the more inward-looking Chuo Line scene, sees younger musicians as wary about travelling outside Japan, whereas the opposite impressions ring true for the Setagaya-ish Aiha Higurashi from Seagull Screaming Kiss Her Kiss Her.

Why such similar music is divided specifically along these lines is difficult to say. Obviously English speakers are more likely to be among those who have connections with bands and labels overseas, and the more connections with overseas a scene has, the less likely it is that its members will accept some of the deeply rooted but unfair and illogical-seeming business practices that the live circuit throws up. A growing sense among younger musicians that the traditional live house way of doing business doesn't afford them the path to prosperity it promises may also feed into an unwillingness to play the game.

It's tempting to say that the Setagaya-type bands are on the right side of history when it comes to their attitude towards technology and their relationship to touring and the economics of live performance. At the same time though, the Chuo Line bands offer dedication and musical innovation that also contributes to the overall health of the music scene. In an ideal world, bands from both backgrounds would mesh at shows into a beautiful rainbow of artistic synthesis. In practice, however, booking bands from both these scenes together is a nightmare. Scenesters won't go out to a show unless they know their mates will all be there. Fans of a band will only come out in enough numbers if they know several other bands on the lineup as well, so mixing up the lineup of an event featuring four or five bands guarantees you're going to disappoint someone. I've personally thrown away more money than I care to think of trying to buck this trend with a mixed lineup. When it fails to come off, it's frustrating beyond words, but when it works, it's magnificent.

OVERCOMING THE SCENE'S LIMITATIONS

It's 8:30pm and I'm at Club Goodman in Akihabara. At this time, in 2008, Goodman is probably the venue that, more than any other in Tokyo, consistently books the bands I most want to see. It's also a place that, whenever I'm there, instantly has me feeling at my most gauche and socially incapable.

Feeling awkward as usual, I cling to the bar, tipping liquid relaxation down my throat to build up the courage I will later need to penetrate the walls of backs, facing out at me in tortoise formation, that will form among the attendees during the lulls between bands. However, this only makes me even more gauche, even less socially capable – a vicious spiral that I choose not to recognise at this time. I'm feeling doubly disheartened at the moment after some poor attendances at my own events, and have a gnawing sense that people don't take me seriously: that they see me as an arrogant, clumsy interloper trying to drunkenly impose a self-centred musical vision on a scene that just doesn't want what I have to sell. I know I need to make nice with these people, but maybe I need to be more accommodating, give them more of what they want. Maybe I'm being too dogmatic.

The band is rattling through some propulsive, synth-led, gothic-neon new wave and the beat is starting to get to me. The gears of my enjoyment by now thoroughly lubricated, by the end of their set I'm convinced that I've just seen the best band in Japan.

I recognise a girl standing near me as another local event organiser. I catch her eye and a babble of superlatives enthuse forth from my mouth.

"Ah, that band was very Ian-type, wasn't it!" she remarks by way of reply.

I'm fairly sure from the context that the underlying message here is, "I disagree with you, but then they were the sort of rubbish you're into I suppose," and I'm starting to fantasise about the sharp response I might swing back at her if I had the courage, but then I realise I'd have no idea what to say. I've been to several of her events and seen some good bands and some bad ones, but I have no idea what kind of music she likes: her shows have no visible identity.

Thinking about this further, I consider that if someone dislikes my shows in a specific and identifiable way, and the flipside of that is that there must be some hypothetical people who could conceivably like them for those same reasons. In any case, it's enough to make me feel I'm on the right track. Pushing aside my doubts about my own activities I decide to double down on what I'm doing.

The fragmented nature of the music scene makes it difficult to do something that doesn't fit the mould, but there are some things you can do to work round it. One is to bring in a ringer.

Basically what this means is reaching outside the scene and paying a more famous band to come in and headline. The advantage a ringer brings to the table is obviously a larger, but also importantly a *broader* fanbase, meaning that people from different scenes will be into them. Unfortunately, there are a couple of problems that go along with this.

Firstly, there is an inverse correlation between the status of a band and the amount of effort they tend to put into promoting a show. Small bands are used to venues taking their money and doing next to nothing to promote them, but bands who are more in demand by promoters are naturally used to other people taking care of that. For a small indie/underground organiser who will likely be promoting among a fairly introverted crowd, a famous headliner's value lies less in their own audience than in how it can boost the audiences other bands bring. Choosing a headliner that will appeal to fans of all or most of the other artists you're booking is key.

Secondly, even if you can use a ringer as a unifying element to bring in an audience drawn from two separate scenes, there is a tendency for fans of one group of bands to cut themselves off from fans of the other bands, hugging opposite sides of the room, or retreating to the corridors or nearby ramen shops when anything unfamiliar is on. This can wreck the atmosphere of an event.

The other thing you can do is just play the long game. Get a cheap venue, book your shows at the same place at regular intervals, get a small crowd of DJs and keep booking the best bands you can, then try to build up an identity and eventually an audience of your own for the party. It's common practice for events in Japan to number themselves Volume 1, Volume 2, Volume 3 and so forth with the idea that the higher the number, the more serious the event appears. Most events never make it past Volume 3, but some like experimental music lab Test Tone and the legendary Toxic Punk Waste events made it to a hundred or more before calling it quits.

Promotion is a tricky one. Venues themselves rarely do much, which is perhaps understandable when they have thirty shows a month to deal with, so it's really up to the bands or the organiser to ensure anyone comes.

Flyers are still a very popular method, and I remember when I first started trying to put on shows being given the rough formula of ten thousand flyers equals one hundred audience. This is a load of rubbish: as a general rule flyers bounce off people like peashooters off a tank. In an admittedly not very scientific 2011 survey of music fans carried out by the venue Ikebukuro Music.org, only 2% of respondents said they got information about gigs from flyers – only the music press ranked as a comparably worthless source of information. Artists' web sites were the main source at 45%, with social media a distant second at 23%. These figures have surely changed in the interim, but the broad picture it paints is of a very decentralised promotional environment in which audiences can be very difficult to coax out to see new or unknown music.

There is obviously a lot of variation in the relative effectiveness of different ways of distributing flyers. Personally and individually giving them to people at a concert will be more effective than the other common Japanese strategy of including them in a thick bundle of flyers that people get offered as they enter shows. While surveys might indicate that flyers aren't a primary source of information, they can be useful for reinforcing in people's minds that a certain event is coming up, and having a pocketful of this paper ammunition is still highly recommended whenever a promoter is out and about socially.

In any case, Japanese bands and organisers still spend a lot of time and money making what are occasionally quite gorgeous flyers. The appeal of the flyer, like listing what "volume" the event is, seems to just come down to making a band or organiser look serious: the flyer serves as visible sign that one is making an effort, even if it's dreadfully inefficient and mostly futile. For bands and regular events, however, there is the additional value of asserting visual identity with art and design. From Peter Saville's iconic work with Factory Records right down to the smallest Tokyo punk or twee pop event, the confluence of music and design is important.

When I started organising events of my own, I struggled, losing money pretty much consistently for several years, kept going only by bloody-minded persistence and a sort of arrogant conviction that my events were the only shows in the city that were really worth doing.

Bloody-mindedness may be the engine that kept driving me onwards against all common sense, but co-operation and collaboration with others is the fuel that keeps the engine running. A key moment for me was when I started running a monthly music night at a local Koenji bar with a friend James Hadfield (the Tokyo-based music journalist, not the man acquitted of high treason by reason of insanity after he attempted to assassinate King George III). The resulting party, Fashion Crisis, despite its naff name, did a number of things right and probably helped me a lot.

Firstly, the Fashion Crisis event worked because it was cheap.

Free initially, although the venue eventually asked us to institute a nominal fee. This low cost removed an important psychological barrier to overcome for entry. We didn't demand any special commitment from guests, which meant they could drop by for one drink and leave, or they could stick around and talk, and it was entirely up to them.

Secondly, being at a fixed, regular time helped foster a regular crowd. We moved the schedule around a bit at first, but eventually we settled on the first Friday of every month. On weekdays, things really were a bit too dead, and on Saturdays people were more likely to have specific, committed plans – not to mention there were often shows *I* wanted to attend elsewhere – but on Friday nights, it could become a monthly ritual for a number of local Chuo train line people on their ways home from work. They always knew the event would be there, it wasn't asking them to cough up 2,000 yen just to walk through the door, and after a while, they knew other people there too.

The event also benefitted from a relaxed and open booking policy. We had live acts some months but not always. The bar, Koenji One, wasn't really a live music space so we could only book acoustic or electronic acts, but we were always open for people to mess around and do new things. The DJ booking was similarly easygoing. We gave musician friends who had never DJed before the chance to play, and we brought in people better known for other events, we let people make mistakes and every month the timetable fell apart in chaos – but importantly, all the people involved were deeply passionate about and knowledgeable about music. I know this is a cliché – "We're *passionate* about music, maaaan!" – and every cheesy corporate event and money-grubbing music business claims it (yeah, sure you are, just like Hitler was *passionate* about the Treaty of Versailles) but there's a lot of very real passion in the Tokyo music scene that often gets lost under the external frivolities. With Fashion Crisis, we tried to throw away the fashion and embrace the crisis.

The end result was that over a period of seven years until the venue's closure, Fashion Crisis managed to foster a regular audience of people who were seriously into music but also, due to the fluid and mixed musical background, were friendly, open-minded and welcoming to casual visitors, without so much of the cliqueyness that can plague the more scene-specific events. Keeping it like that is a constant challenge, as cliques will tend to grow up of their own accord wherever they can lay root, but we did OK. No one made any money out of it apart from the building's landlords, and if any of us had, it would have put a wedge into the relationship between us and the regulars. Instead, what we ended up with was a small community of our own.

Now my own personal musical activity had always been far more specific, even militant, in its musical focus than the easygoing Fashion Crisis nights – I wouldn't be able to charge real money for something as loose as that, and an important part of its appeal was that we didn't. However, once you're asking people to part with serious cash to see an event, I think you owe it to them to be clear in your own mind about what it is that you're offering.

What the Fashion Crisis community did end up giving me, however, was a kind of hinterland that formed the basis of the audience for my other shows, and, if not actually improving my precarious financial state much, at least mitigated the damage as my own taste fell further and further out of sync with the indie scene's prevailing currents. Sometimes, on an especially good night, I might even come close to breaking even, so the natural next step was to wipe out all that financial progress in one grand gesture and start my own label.

KILL YOUR LABEL

While organising events throughout Tokyo, I began to pour massive amounts of money that I really should have been saving for my future and having children into Call And Response Records. Releasing a couple of CDs a year from bands I liked, along with occasional compilations where I reached out wider into the scene, I gradually drew around me a core of musicians who could represent my grand project. Call And Response was to be a labour of love, and like all great love affairs, it began in a dizzying whirl of romantic ideals and no practical consideration about how things would work in the long-term. Promotion, advertising and media relations were fleeting concerns, for example, when I had the important business of catalogue numbers to consider.

One thing that always amused me was the way that indie bands self-releasing their own albums would give their albums three-figure catalogue numbers like "XQD-001" – as if they were *ever* going to put out more than a hundred releases on that label. As a private joke to myself, I numbered my first release CAR-99 and started counting down towards zero, at which point I told myself that, like my hometown of Bristol's legendary Sarah

Records, I would slam down the shutters, say thank you and no more. It would be like lightning: dazzling, white hot and gone in a flash. I congratulated myself on how romantic and punk rock I was, until I did some calculations and realised that even with the frequent limited-run CD/Rs and free downloads I was doing between main releases it would take me thirty years to get to the point where I could drop my mic and exit stage right.

The intervening decades, however, were set to be a decidedly unromantic grind in the face of public indifference and my own incompetence. The only thing keeping me going was a combination of sheer terror of looking stupid with the now rather quixotic looking reverse catalogue numbering system I had saddled myself with, and my obsessive, possessive, and not a little desperate love for the music.

Much as I might complain about the drain on my resources that running a label represents, historically speaking, producing and pressing an album in this day and age has never been cheaper or easier. When indie labels began to appear in the mid-80s, owners had to overcome massive production costs, either through sheer business acumen or blind, bludgeoning persistence. As in the West, though, the definition of "indie" in the specific context of record labels is not always clear-cut. I spoke with Yui Kimijima, a recording engineer at Tsubame Studios and guitarist of post-rock/art-punk band Gaji, and he explained some of the distinctions.

"There are two types of indies that have been there from the start," says Kimijima, "You have indies as a pre-matured or 'would-be' form of the professional music industry; and then you have indies in a much more unorganized and art-oriented form. The former is in a dependent relationship with the majors – perhaps contrary to what the word 'indie' implies – in terms of A&R strategy and finance. The latter is an autonomous ecosystem of bands, fans, distro and shops, as you can see with the harsh noise scene over the past thirty years. As the majors have declined, the former type of indie has almost ceased to exist as a sub-system of music industry, perhaps for a decade or more now,"

The decline of these indie "feeder labels" with links to majors has left small DIY labels, chaotically run by either bands themselves or enthusiasts and dilettantes like me, as the main type – and enthusiasts make much better customers than they do businessmen. As with the live scene, the shape of the business has inverted to place these bands and enthusiasts not in the role of workers but as consumers of music-related services. As someone who, as both a musician and an engineer, has experience on both sides of this relationship, Kimijima offers an interesting perspective.

"Indie music has become more and more an informal sector or an underground economy than that was in the 90s," he explains, "It persists based on how much people have in their pockets, not the size of the budget the A&R person from the sub-sub-contractor label of the music business giant is responsible for. Nowadays, more and more indie musicians and label owners have a day job. They pay me out of their salary. I doubt all of them register the expenses of recording in their tax reports or any formal declarations. Basically, a certain portion of money simply vanishes from the formal economy and flows into the underground – which I don't think is necessarily a bad thing at all!"

Even as those indies run along traditional business lines have begun to shrink out of existence, costs for dilettante enthusiasts like me, or more often for bands' own self-released records, have come down, expanding access to this informal economy of music-related services. As with the music press and the live circuit, there are companies out there monetising every possible aspect of the record production process – as well as a growing array of equivalent services provided in a DIY capacity by other people within the same ecosystem – and those bands willing to fork out can relatively easily take control of the whole process themselves. Recording studio? Check. Engineer? Check. Mixing and mastering? Check. CD press? Check. Distribution? Check. You can put together and release into shops a fairly professional looking and sounding album with no interference from a label, so why does a label need to exist?

Well, one reason is laziness. A lot of bands just don't want the hassle of organising all that stuff, so having a label take care of it is a huge weight off their shoulders.

Another reason is cost. All those services add up to a hell of a lot of money. Studio time, and especially the engineers, vary a lot in cost but can run to hundreds of thousands of yen for an eight-song mini-album. The cost of pressing five hundred or a thousand CDs runs to about a 100,000 yen or thereabouts, depending on options. A young band will be very lucky to find a label willing and able to pay all of those costs, but any decent label will at least take on part of the expense.

Lastly, there is the value of identity. When there are bajillions of bands self-releasing new albums or just dumping them onto the web week after week after week, and with the record stores that used to play the roles of tastemakers, as in the Shibuya-*kei* era, in decline, labels have a valuable role as curators. They filter music not just in terms of subjective measures like quality, but also in terms of simply matching together music that shares common characteristics or points of appeal.

Once actually in the studio, it's worth taking a moment for a bit of an East-West compare-and-contrast session, because the behaviour, culture and habits of musicians in the Japanese indie scene work in a few subtle ways towards creating an end product with its own distinct characteristics.

Seb Roberts, an engineer who has worked with bands in North America as well as in Japan, points out that, with all the usual caveats for the rich pageant of different personalities that the musical spectrum presents, the working relationship between the band and engineer tends to be rather different.

"Japanese bands are much more deferential to engineers as 'experts' in their field," says Roberts, "Western bands may happily shrug and admit they don't understand what's going on, but that doesn't stop them from sharing their aesthetic judgment in the same moment. Because Western musicians tend to be (excuse my French) bigger assholes as a habit, any poor creative decisions they insist upon are more likely to make in onto the record. Let me put it this way: any really shitty mixes I've heard on Japanese albums, I can usually pin the blame squarely on the engineer."

This deference to engineers' expertise, perhaps combined with Japanese bands' generally far more diligent attitude towards rehearsal and professionalism, can extend to a greater patience with the more arcane and esoteric aspects of the recording process (as Roberts explains, "They'll let me spend an hour A/B-ing mics or finding the drummer's 'sweet spot'") although it can also leave them at the mercy of some studio habits common among many Japanese engineers.

While some of the engineering issues Japanese music faces mirror those in the west (Kimijima complains, "I think we are losing headroom. Recordings are getting too loud, pushed too hard to the digital clip point"), Roberts singles out a tendency in Japanese rock for mastering that is "way too hot", with the snare compressed to the point where it sounds like a timbale and the hi-hat far louder than good taste should ever require.

"The mixes are comparatively bright overall," Roberts adds, "Super treble-heavy mixes have always been the province of dance music in the west, while rock was always a very mid-forward genre. In Japan, a lot of records can sound quite shrill."

Part of the reason for Japan's tilt towards more treble-heavy mixes may be the result of engineers needing to fill the space between the instrumentation and vocals that in Japan tend to fall in a higher register, especially with female singers.

In any case, once the recording, mixing and mastering processes have been navigated, the end result for most indie bands is usually a CD with about seven songs, running to about

161

30 minutes in length. The reasons that these kinds of mini-albums dominate probably lie partly in how the format balances recording costs against record stores' dislike of non-idol CD singles and low-priced EPs. Additionally, and perhaps more importantly, both bands and audiences are trained by the live scene's standard 30-minute set times to deliver and digest music in these concise chunks. With the music being developed in this environment, it is perhaps natural that the tendency is to document it in a similar form.

Whatever the reasons, I speak without hyperbole when I say that the perfection of the mini-album is – all technical quibbles aside – the single greatest artistic achievement the Japanese indie music economy has given the 21st Century music scene. In the early days of vinyl, a sweet, concise 30-35 minutes was the standard length for an album, something that the rise of the CD in the 1990s ruined with a grim slide into flabby self-indulgence (as Roberts succinctly interjects: "*Mellon Collie and the Infinite Sadness*? Are you fucking kidding, Billy?!?") In fact, while parts of the Western media back in 2013 tied themselves in idiotic knots, attempting to spin a temporary blip in sales caused by the idol scene's bubble economy as the rebirth of CDs, a more artistically inclined observer might look instead to the Japanese indie scene for a saviour – if not of the format's commercial life, at least of its soul.

YES, BUT WHY ARE YOU TALKING ABOUT CDs?

It's midnight and two young men peer out furtively from round the corner. They'd had a fright a little earlier when a policeman had trundled past on the squeaking wheels of his bicycle, but there's no sign of him now. The third member of their little criminal enterprise gives them the all-clear from across the road and they shuffle across as fast as they can with the heavy load they carry between them.

The last houses are behind them now, with only the rough, gravel and grass expanse between them and the mostly dry riverbed. Their friend joins them to help shift the enormous package now and they're able to make quicker progress.

What's that sound? Is the cop making his rounds again? No, just a drunk businessman plotting a winding path down the empty road. If the cop is still around, hopefully that guy will occupy his attention.

They make it to the riverbank and place the package down at the top of the small slope as they catch their breath. They look down at the jagged shadows of long grass, taking in the sound of running water that they can't quite see. They don't want to do this — it seems such a sordid deed, such a betrayal of love — but there's no choice: they can't keep it in their dorm. They each place their foot on the package so that no single one of them is to blame, and they push.

The package tumbles down the bank, reaching the bottom with a loud

crash that has them looking around in alarm lest anyone have spotted them.
Their eyes meet and they nod. Time to scatter.

They run off in different directions, making their way back to their
student dorm by prepared routes. Meanwhile, the package lies where they left
it, split open at the bottom of the bank, spilling out onto the dry riverbed its
cargo: five hundred copies of idol group AKB48's single Sayonara Crawl.

One of the big changes that I've watched from afar since I
moved to Japan in 2001 has been the utter and complete
disintegration of the Western CD market. This is something I've
followed with a curious sense of detachment, because in Japan
there was no parallel collapse. The music market as a whole has
been on a more or less uninterrupted trajectory of decline since
about 1998, but there was for a long time no related
technological disruption with the music industry uploading itself
into cyberspace and physical media being left to rot.

Primarily, this was the result of business practices right at the
top, in particular at Sony. Sony Music occupies an extremely
influential position in the Japanese music industry, but it is still
part of the wider Sony Group. Within Sony there is a culture of
almost fanatical devotion to audio fidelity, and more importantly
than that, a large part of its consumer electronics business has
relied for a long time on the sales of CD players. As a result,
distaste for the MP3 format and internal pressure designed to
support Sony's consumer electronics division kept Sony Music
out of the downloads market until late 2011, and with such a vast
catalogue of artists locked out, it couldn't help but stymie the
development of the legal music download industry.

While Sony is often portrayed as the villain of the piece who prevents the music industry from adapting, the truth is that all major labels are highly conservative in that regard, even compared to their Western equivalents. Avex are often presented as the good guys, the newcomers barging into the staid old world of industry fossils and shaking things up with their youthful vibrancy and fresh ideas, but their behaviour with regard to sites like YouTube has also been decidedly conservative. The Johnny & Associates boy band talent agency takes it several steps further, to the point where even record stores and the Oricon chart company are forbidden from showing the CD jackets of Johnny's artists on their web sites, while publishers are forced to grey out the faces of Johnny's artists when they post their magazine covers online.

What it comes down to is the way the big labels and talent agencies are used to exerting complete control over every aspect of the market, monetising in their favour every interaction between the various players: not only with music sales but also radio airplay, music video broadcasts, video and DVD sales, image rights and merchandise. This is true throughout the world, but local conditions saw Western and Japanese companies adopt slightly different tactics to respond to the disruption to the business model wrought by the web.

In America, the music industry mobilised its lawyers and lobbyists to make the legal process by which they could sue and claim damages from illegal downloaders more efficient. They turned the process of sending out writs into a business in and of itself. In Japan, companies simply closed ranks behind the existing business model and carried on as before, as if by sheer force of will alone they could send time into reverse.

Because CDs in Japan are very profitable, with a CD album by a major label act still often costing around 3,000 yen, they can make far greater profits off physical media than from downloads. In fact, while in the West the CD has gone the way of the quagga, Stellar's sea cow and the notion of shame in American politics, in Japan a jump in CD sales actually propelled the music industry into a period of growth which saw the Japanese music market temporarily replace the United States as the world's largest in 2012.

But of course there's a snag.

The snag is that those CD sales were concentrated in two main areas: singles by idol groups and hit compilations by golden oldies. The hits and reissues market is really just playing off past successes and its audience most likely skews older, so it's hard to find any model where those sales are sustainable in the long-term. Meanwhile, much of the sales figures racked up by contemporary idol groups are built on a business model based around hardcore fans buying multiple copies of the same CD in return for access to the group members and participation in special events.

The truth is that growth, where it has come with companies like Avex, has been largely the result of companies finding new things besides music to monetise: through visual media tie-ups and what we might term character goods. What the massive CD sales of idol groups like AKB48 represent is the transformation of the CD from a medium for delivering music into a symbol sanctifying the completion of a purchasing act designed to express love. While CD sales have held up better in Japan than elsewhere due to conservative industry groupthink and the major labels' ability to control the marketplace, some of its reported successes are a bit misleading. Industry figures for 2013 proved that 2012 had been a blip, with a sharp correction that resumed the downward trend.

In any case, the big profits are only being accrued at the very top, with a handful of acts, many reliant on defiantly unmusical and exploitative marketing gimmicks to prop up their sales, raking in the lion's share of the cash and most of the rest flowing in from back catalogue and reissues. As far as indie music is concerned, most bands find themselves still cast in the role of consumer, with a host of people, from the live venues to the CD production businesses to the music press and even some labels to a certain extent, sucking money out of them on the vague promise of something further down the line.

Meanwhile the indie CD market itself has remained in a state of glacially slow decline, noticeable in the gradual disappearance of record shops. Nevertheless, CDs are increasingly being challenged as the medium by which bands distribute their music. Web sites like Bandcamp serve as alternatives to CDs along with a belated boarding of the vinyl and cassette revivalist bandwagon. Indie bands are also following Avex's lead and realising that merchandise needn't stop with t-shirts and badges either. Some artists have turned themselves into quite successful little brands, with their music and live performances increasingly functioning as BGM and sales presentations for the real business of flogging tote bags with faux-naïve drawings on the side.

Still, no matter what goods bands peddle for financial sustainability, to draw audiences they need to be able to communicate, and in this they must face the age-old choice about language.

LANGUAGE AND JAPANESENESS

The house lights drop and a single blue spotlight casts a cold illumination over a girl with a guitar. Her face mostly hidden behind a long fringe, she fiddles about with a few of her effects pedals, strums out a couple of atonal non-chords and makes a sort of coughing sound into the mic to check everything is working.

She should really have sorted out this stuff before going onstage. In fact I saw her checking all these things while she was setting up just five minutes ago. It's just nerves, performance anxiety, superstition that makes her check them again once she's exposed under the spotlight. It's working though, so now she starts to play for real.

Her voice murmurs over a fragile melody, the guitar treated with a layer of fuzz but nonetheless possessed of an understated, glacial beauty. In the background, a drummer brushes minimally across the skins, while a violin adds its yearning lament to the song. Barely more than a whisper, she continues to sing, the words taunting me on the edge of comprehension. I recognise a bit here and there, fragments of English phrases seeming to slip in and out of the washes of chords and textures, while other parts might be Japanese or even some made-up language that exists only to put into words the alien yet strangely familiar sonic dreamscape. Whatever they are, they are surely saying something ineffably beautiful.

I pick up the girl's self-released CD/R on the way out, its naïve,
faintly surreal, hand-drawn artwork seeming to come from the same place,
just beyond the edge of reality, as the music. It has a lyrics sheet as well, so as
the CD whirs round and the same sparse but richly suggestive music seeps
out of the speakers and starts to fill the room around me, I begin to read.

After a couple of minutes, I put the booklet down and try to forget
about what I've read, but it's too late. The last track was a love song, and in
this next one she's singing about her feelings. Her feelings are banal, and her
English is clearly not a sophisticated enough tool to express them in any
imaginative or creative way. I don't know what the next song is about, but
the mystique has vanished. I should never have looked.

As a general rule, a Japanese artist wanting to achieve mainstream
success in their domestic market must sing in Japanese. There are
a number of reasons for this, and they cover both commercial
and artistic fields.

Firstly, there's the issue of communication. In order for
audiences to understand musicians and relate to their messages,
it's helpful if listeners can follow the language. In spite of all that
musicians have to say about the universal language of music and
despite the vaunted subtlety of the Japanese language in the fast-
paced disposable world of pop and rock, people will rarely put
the effort into trying to understand something that doesn't state
its intentions directly.

It also makes more commercial sense to sing dreary, insipid
love ballads in Japanese so that once people hear how much
musicians value friendship, peace and joy, they will be inspired in
the deepest pits of their wallets. If they can understand the lyrics,

they will be more easily able to sing the songs at karaoke and their friends will be able to cry over them at weddings. The easier and simpler something is, the less work people need to put into understanding it, and since pop aims for wide demographics, the dumbing-down that usually goes hand-in-hand with mass appeal inherently favours a native language.

But language doesn't just embody meanings of individual words; it also embodies thought processes, and these aren't always mutually and directly transferrable. Language can be seen as a set of rails on which thoughts can travel, and different sets of rails carry thoughts to slightly different places. There are cultural and social concepts that are deeply embedded in the Japanese language that don't exist in English, so if a Japanese songwriter wants to write honestly and clearly about their life, world and experience, they will often need to be able to do it in nuanced Japanese. So not only the dumbing-down aspects of capitalism, but also the expressive and enlightening aspects of art can favour native language pop.

Globalised art forms are adapted to local cultural contexts that bend and mutate foreign aesthetic structures. It was a big deal in the Soviet Union when Andrei Makarevich of Time Machine (*Mashina Vremeni*) found a way of singing rock music in Russian, but it was also a big deal when The Beatles and especially The Kinks found ways of singing rock'n'roll in not just British but specifically regional British vernacular. Taking an art form and adapting it in a way that speaks to local circumstances is a very powerful thing and one of the foundation stones that helps build and maintain a sense of national identity.

However, in Japan and elsewhere many musicians still prefer to sing in English, so it's worth considering why that is too.

While Japanese is very good at expressing "Japanese-like" thoughts, the inverse of that is that it's rather bad at expressing thoughts that don't travel along those rails, and many artists enjoy the freedom that a foreign language gives them in being able to let their thoughts float free of such semantic restrictions. Aiha Higurashi of Seagull Screaming Kiss Her Kiss Her told me about her attraction to the English language's flexibility.

"English words are more musical," she explains, "They're like percussion, like piano, like guitar riffs. I can put English words over my piano or riffs more easily. If I think about writing Japanese, it's really hard – I have to think from one word to another, how this word goes well or this word doesn't go well so I have to change it, or it doesn't make any sense. But I can really write freely in English."

Whether a native English speaker would necessarily take such a loose approach to the language is perhaps a matter of debate, but as we have already seen, there are certainly ways that the Japanese language can be challenging to fit into pop and rock rhythms and melodies. In contrast, English tends to permit a more conversational style – Higurashi cites Thurston Moore and Lou Reed in particular as vocalists whose "talking style" she finds particularly appealing.

The source of one's influences is of course very important when it comes to the language a musician sings in too. In a *Japan Times* interview I did several years ago with Minami Yamaguchi from indiepop/postpunk act She Talks Silence, she explained that because most of the music she listened to was sung in English, English felt the most natural language for her to use. This is essentially the position that Yuya Uchida was advocating forty years ago, and it's one that's never going to go away. As long as new music keeps appearing in the West, there are going to be first-adopters in Japan for whom the English language feels like a more natural fit.

Sometimes English works its way into mostly Japanese-language singles as a form of punctuation. Pop musicians often pepper their songs with boilerplate English phrases that are used to express more or less nothing, with phrases like "stand by me" or "hold my hand" interrupting streams of Japanese and functioning primarily as rhythmical placeholders. Meanwhile, punk bands often find that English is a more effective language for blunt sloganeering – after all, everyone knows what "Fuck you!" means. In these examples, English is really functioning as an adjunct to the Japanese language and its intended impact still relies on being understood by Japanese speaking listeners.

For success outside of Japan, some musicians and industry figures believe that writing lyrics in English increases one's chances of hitting it big abroad. This tactic has worked for Swedish songwriters and producers, who since the late-90s have exerted a massively disproportionate influence on the global pop scene, thanks to their ability to absorb new trends and distill them into their catchiest form. Needless to say, the English language is still more or less a prerequisite for global chart-topping success (do not even *think* of mentioning Korean novelty hit *Gangnam Style* here) and so the logic follows that Japanese artists who sing in English are at an advantage.

Groups like YMO and Shonen Knife almost certainly benefitted from singing in English or producing English versions of their songs – the former working with lyricist Chris Mosdell to produce a professional end result and the latter's clumsy English working as a counterpart to the naïve charm and offbeat creativity of their music. That was decades ago though, and it is questionable the extent to which that approach has value nowadays. Firstly, while Japan's domestic music market is broadly in decline, it has so far held up better than that of many other countries. Why would an artist invest the time and money in producing and promoting English language material abroad when the market that already exists on their doorstep is so much more promising? Secondly, the appeal of Japanese artists who have claimed meaningful overseas fanbases over the past ten years has tended to be visual in nature, either in the case of visual-*kei*, which seems to have carved out a sort of zombie existence in the West, particularly France, long after its commercial death in Japan, or in visually stylised acts like Kyary Pamyu Pamyu and Perfume. Fans of these acts don't really need to understand the lyrics and in fact often prefer the "correct" original Japanese. In any case, translations are not hard to come by online.

While singing in English might be commercially beneficial to some bands who are able to carve out a niche in a foreign market, usually the strategy is more trouble than it's worth. Japanese bands' use of English lyrics doesn't always play well with overseas listeners, who can find badly done English distracting at best and at worst embarrassing to hear. To many, the attraction of Japanese music is precisely because of its Japaneseness, and so fans would rather not have the bands try to communicate with them in English: for them the words should remain shrouded in Oriental mystery. This view is particularly understandable among pop fans given how utterly, incorrigibly dreadful basically all J-Pop lyrics are.

Criticisms against Japanese vocalists using English also arise from within the local scene, with the argument that "Japanese should sing in Japanese" often sitting at the core. The implication underlying this is that singing in a foreign language is elitist and pretentious. Back in 1979, new wave legends P-Model skewered the way people accepted received notions of imported things being inherently cool with cynical glee in the song *Sophisticated*. The song is ironically sung in English and the final self-effacing line goes, "Sophisticated, the foreign language song."*

Back in the 70s and 80s, when *Sophisticated* was written, there certainly was an elitist notion that cool or sophistication was something imported and handed down by privileged experts. Elements of this persisted into the 90s, and were visibly at work in the Shibuya-*kei* scene.

However, by the end of the 90s, subcultural groups were rejecting foreign elitism en masse, while the mainstream was becoming far more confident in its Japaneseness. The *gyaru* girls' street fashion movement and otaku subcultures in particular did

---

* One probably shouldn't take P-Model's satire too seriously; their producer, Masahide Sakuma, was also a member of their contemporaries the Plastics, nearly all of whose songs were in English.

175

an effective job of removing cultural elites from the pop and fashion landscapes, while in music the commercial juggernaut of J-Pop was increasingly marginalising foreign artists. The market's eager co-option and repackaging of *gyaru* and otaku culture has subsequently ensured that Japanese language music has full spectrum dominance of the industry. In this environment, taking the position of a plucky fighter against elitist oppression when criticising a foreign language song starts to look like nothing more than anti-intellectual, nationalistic bullying.

National identity nevertheless maintains a strong hold over how people relate to popular culture, and social context is a complex thing. In the same interview, She Talks Silence's Minami Yamaguchi suggested that, "Perhaps it's the impact of the [March 11th, 2011] earthquake, but recently you get a lot of people praising music sung in Japanese and criticising Japanese bands who sing in English."

Language is one of the key ways in which we anchor ourselves in society, from the slang that helps define regional identity to the national language that unites nations. The social impact of the 2011 earthquake, tsunami and nuclear disaster was wide and deep, and one of its most immediate manifestations was in the need to seek out the reassurance of shared bonds between people. The word for that, which achieved totemic significance that year, was *kizuna*. While *kizuna* is a treasure of the Japanese language, it can also lead to a situation that becomes dogmatic and intolerant of those who refuse to conform or extend that bond. In the long run, any such dogma is bad for art. Japanese music needs these first-adopters and iconoclasts to lay the groundwork from which Japanese music can develop and remain a living thing. If, from their work, others can work out ways of adapting and expressing it in a native idiom, then that's to be applauded, but Japanese should be wary of Orientalising themselves by making these exclusive cultural prescriptions of what "Japanese music" should be and do. That way only leads to the creative mummification of *enka*.

The heated debate on language in Japanese rock, which raged in the 1970s, has cooled off, and even the national anxiety precipitated by the 2011 disaster has begun to fade. For mainstream music, Japanese has won a clear and decisive victory over English. Where foreign languages can still be found, it is at peripheral intersections, with artists preparing their work for export or artists at the first stage of parsing new imports. Any linguistic debate that remains is one about the extent to which an artist *should* channel their art through these native pop and rock traditions, the extent to which an artist *should* be influenced by foreign music. Now that the practicalities of making Japanese rock and pop have been largely worked through, the question of language is less aesthetic than political in nature, and politics is an issue with broader implications that go far beyond language.

ALL ART IS POLITICAL

The band members are wearing kimonos, but their hair is a mishmash of punk styles. They bounce around the stage, pounding out a traditional Japanese festival rhythm on taiko drums while the guitars churn through a mixture of ska-punk and squalls of noise. The audience is caught up in the festival spirit, fists punching the air. The vocalist lifts his own fist into the air and screams about honouring lost Japanese soldiers at Yasukuni Shrine*.

As a lone foreigner in a crowd of furiously pogoing punk kids, this moment sucks all the life and energy out of the experience and I start the slink back through the crowd towards the corner of the room. This is clearly a bonding ritual that I'm not meant to be at the centre of, and observing from the fringes is where I feel most comfortable now anyway.

Nevertheless, looking around me as I drift backwards through the undulating sea of people, I can see anarcho-punks, liberal university band club nerds, plainly apolitical kids who were just out for a party – all enjoying

---

* Yasukuni Shrine is sometimes visited by politicians to honour Japan's war dead. The religious site in Tokyo became the centre of political disputes with many of Japan's neighbours, as well as a Mecca for neofascists and right-wingers, since a number of convicted Class A war criminals were enshrined there.

the show together, all bonded by a shared sense of identity, even as they parse the music's message in subtly different ways.

Nationalism is a loaded word, and tends to put people quickly on the defensive, but the patterns of thought it describes are important in helping us understand pop culture, both in Japan and abroad.

Growing up in the UK just as bands like Oasis and Blur were peaking, I was slow to realise just how nationalistic this Britpop era's underlying ethos really was. There was a cheeky swagger and self-deprecating irony to the "British is Best" ideology these bands expounded, and I didn't yet see how that light-hearted edge deflected criticism and allowed a damaging and dangerous message to slip through unchallenged.

As a response to the invasion of grunge from the United States, Britpop seemed to be about an anti-globalist reclamation of national – and more than that, specifically local and regional – identity in the face of a sort of homogenising corporate creep that many of us at the time associated with America. If it sometimes tipped over into outright anti-Americanism, it felt harmless because we were the underdogs – plucky Brits in our Spitfires defending our way of life against an implacable foreign menace. I was too young and stupid to notice that the movement carried within it those same forces of capitalist greed, and it was no coincidence that Britpop's dissolution coincided with the newly sanitised, socialism-free Labour Party's victory in the 1997 general election. That was the year the underdog showed its teeth and we started to realise it was rabid. Hey, America, I know we said that stuff, but can you help us out a bit? Can we at least have Radiohead back?

Like Britain did briefly in the 90s, J-Pop has successfully out-branded foreign music in the domestic market, but unlike the mixture of swagger and cynicism that characterised Britpop, the soft-focus vision of Japan J-Pop presents is decidedly banal. It seems domestically branded pop culture can be just as vulnerable to the homogenising effects of the corporate music industry as its globalised (read "Americanised") counterpart. Resistance to this corporate-driven homogeneity can come from traditionally left- or right-wing ideological positions, and it's not uncommon for them to mix.

One particularly revered band in the punk/underground scene is Seppuku Pistols, who combine traditional Japanese taiko and festival music with a rough-edged punk sensibility and a fierce pride in Japan. They've always been an incredibly friendly and welcoming band, and they insist that they are patriotic but not nationalistic; however, such nuanced distinctions are sometimes lost in the simplistic frenzy of a punk rock show. Ostentatious displays of national pride may give a sense of warmth and belonging to someone from within the national group, but they can also heighten consciousness of division between locals and outsiders. There's also something else going on with Seppuku Pistols though, and in their particular brand of patriotic party punk, there is an element of reclaiming national identity from the establishment and allowing outsiders and those on the sidelines to claim ownership of Japaneseness for themselves.

As in my teenage Britpop years, the politics of a thing can depend greatly on the context of a particular audience, and issues that are simplified and entrenched in mainstream discourse are fluid and multi-layered in how they permeate and mutate their way through real life. And with even bands as overt as Seppuku Pistols being consumed apolitically by many, the politics inherent in most Japanese music tends to go entirely unnoticed. Still, it's there and politics runs through everything.

Pop songs are inextricable from the circumstances of their production and circulation, and the more strenuously a musician denies the political nature of their work, the more strongly they underline the nature and extent of their politics.

When most people think of politics and music in Japan, two images traditionally come to mind. One is of singers such as Goro Nakagawa and Nobuyasu Okabayashi, whose acoustic street-folk soundtracked the late-60s student radical movement; the other is the underground rockers of the 1970s, along with their affiliations to radical communist revolutionary groups. This lingering image of the left as dangerous fanatics was cemented by live broadcasts of tragedies like the *Asama-Sansō* hostage incident in the early 70s. At that time, violence erupting from within the left made it appear hypocritical and many artists distanced themselves from it. As the number of radicals declined, a neutered Japanese pop music flowered; old hippies were co-opted into the idol-industrial complex and while some may have had subversive intentions, the overarching understanding was that music didn't *do* politics.

Political issues didn't disappear from music entirely of

course. Kiyoshiro Imawano of the highly acclaimed folk-rock band RC Succession, was pointedly anti-war and anti-nuclear, although even such mild sentiments as those led to trouble with Toshiba EMI resulting in the label dropping the band's 1988 album *Covers* prior to release. The album was later released to great success on another label, and Imawano's influence lingers today, most prominently in the Fuji Rock festival, of which he is something of a patron saint. Other 70s generation artists like Ryuichi Sakamoto have spoken out on similar issues, usually with severe blowback from commercial interests and right wing groups within Japan. While these issues retain support among the general population of Japan, the fact that speaking out on them is considered controversial by the standards of the music industry demonstrates the narrowness of the range of expression the business is set up to handle.

By removing a whole range of subjects and ideas from the realm of the national shared culture, Japanese pop music and the entertainment industry, contribute to a limiting of society's broader capacity for political and social discourse. This doesn't mean Japanese pop isn't political though: far from it. Whether it is intended or not, all art serves someone's politics either through reinforcement, subversion or omission. The most inane love song still deals with interactions between boys and girls, and so the roles taken by the participants can subvert or reinforce gender roles. The way certain AKB48 songs position female group members to sing from the perspective of their male observers tells us something about the odd relationship they have with their fans – in particular how the girls themselves are stripped of agency, positioned so as to observe themselves as objects. You can see this in the way the lyrics of *Ponytail to Shushu* and *Everyday, Kachusha* focus on particular aspects of the subject's appearance – a ponytail in one case and an Alice band in the other. In each case, the girls themselves sing from the male fan's perspective, directing a fetishising focus in on one superficial aspect of the song's female object. In this way, AKB48 fetishise themselves, perhaps simply to save their fans the effort of doing so on their own, or perhaps also to provide tacit legitimisation for the voyeuristic fetishism the fans were already engaged in.

Pop singer Kana Nishino comes from a different background, with her image drawing from a tradition with roots in 1990s *gyaru* culture. In the song *Make Up*, a recently dumped Nishino holds back tears by focusing on the application of cosmetics, painting herself a new mood. The song is embedded with all the contradictions of Nishino's *gyaru* hinterland, which tends to wallow masochistically in the romantic suffering and mistreatment of women even as it reinforces the gender roles that put women in such positions the first place. In the lyrics, Nishino puts on a defiant face, declaring that all she needs are her "best friends and makeup", presenting the makeup as empowering and not for anyone's benefit but her own, adding in a side order of "You go girl!" At the same time, however, the song spends a lot of time wallowing in the tragedy of the woman done wrong, which is rather the stock in trade of *gyaru* literature. The focus on makeup as the agent of rebirth puts commercial beauty products alongside friends as signifiers of identity and belonging.

Similarly, the conflict in Kyary Pamyu Pamyu's hit songs is often resolved through the act of taking what you want – now and without fear of consequences – often in the form of consumer goods. This is a mindset associated with children, who are obviously a big part of Kyary's intended audience, but it also reflects a very particular set of assumptions about what is a desirable kind of life. In debut single *Ponponpon,* the lyrics are about riding a merry-go-round, expressing yourself and creating your own path to follow; Kyary's language all might seem like boilerplate "follow-your-dreams" lifestyle TV platitudes, but that's the point. It is also a hymn to disposability, and while the lyrics hint at something anti-establishment, they are an absolute rejection of rebellion in the 1960s/70s-style socialist sense in favour of this individualistic idea that defines freedom as the freedom to pursue instant gratification. The fact that nearly every Kyary Pamyu Pamyu single since has been written for a TV commercial that helpfully provides suggestions as to how you can achieve that disposable instant gratification right now tells you everything you need to know about the underlying ethos of her star persona, but the seed of that idea was there from the start.

Now that's not to dismiss the aforementioned songs or to use politics as a stick to bash them with – apart from the marvellous *Ponponpon,* they're all dreadful enough on their own musical merits for that not to be necessary. The point is that the idea of "politics" is really much wider than most people allow. Within Japanese music criticism, this consideration is often forgotten. Literary criticism has no such problem, but somehow in pop music politics falls out of bounds – and music is impoverished when this is the case.

Politics in the indie and underground scenes is a tricky beast to pin down. Existing outside the commercial axis that defines mainstream pop, underground and indie music have a broader range of voices. It helps a bit to go back once more to the 1970s, since that was where the underground first really established its voice as something consciously against the mainstream.

The 1970s underground was born out of the struggles of the 1960s student movement and was therefore broadly leftist. This initially carried over into the punk scene, the first generation of which had strong roots in the 1970s underground, but as in the UK, where neofascist skinhead groups started to take over punk gigs, a number of the 80s wave of punks in Japan were of a decidedly right wing, nationalist bent. Some were attracted to the rage and violence inherent in punk but rather than seeing it as transformative, creative destruction, they were attracted to the violence and strength as an end in itself.

There was, as you might suspect, a fair amount of crossover between the neofascist punk scene and the lower echelons of the yakuza, the *chinpira* and street thugs. This continues as a subset of Japanese punk to this day, although largely segregated from the modern day descendants of the 1970s underground, whose politics, lacking any real credible focus, have largely dissipated and fragmented. Underground music may accept a wider range of voices, but the grip the mainstream has over the extent and range of the political spectrum makes it hard for many young musicians to articulate discontent or rebellion. Instead what you find is a lot of interesting and often intelligent fragments of social criticism stitched together in novel ways, but usually with a sense of a distant observer rather than one who sees themselves as actively involved or participating in the world they describe. In this sense, it shares a lot in common with new wave musicians like the Plastics, P-Model and their contemporaries, commenting on society without specifically advocating any particular position.

Most punk simply adopts the imagery of old British music from a purely fashion-based perspective, even down to the black and white photocopied flyers with grainy photos of Margaret Thatcher looking mad and evil on them. Of course there is still plenty of punk eagerly plastering swastikas over pictures of Prime Minister Shinzo Abe's face, peppering their posters with anarcho-syndicalist flags and using the Crass typeface to disseminate gig information. The extent to which they understand the imagery they're using isn't always clear, but the intention is still heartening. And a thread of genuine, old-school left-anarchist communalism remains, with strong roots in particular in the Koenji area and close links with the music scene. It was through the Koenji punk grapevine that I learned ahead of media reports of the 2012 release from prison of Pussy Riot's Yekaterina Samutsevich, the word having gone out via the Voina anarchist artists' collective through to the European squatters' communes and Japanese underground activist networks. It was these same networks, with their connections to the punk scene, that were the initial driving force behind the anti-nuclear protests that sprang up in the wake of the 2011 Fukushima nuclear disaster.

One shouldn't make the mistake of equating Japanese anti-authoritarian protest and social criticism with its Western equivalents though. Traditionally left-wing positions can often sit side by side with positions generally considered the property of the right. Central to all this is the fact that Japan is still essentially a nation living under foreign occupation seventy years after its defeat in the Second World War. Due to the ever-present American military occupation, anti-nuclear and anti-war positions have always dovetailed with nationalism in a way that would sit far less comfortably in Britain or America. Protests against or criticisms of the establishment are necessarily criticisms in some way of the United States. America is the elephant in the room, and it muddles traditional left-right dichotomies, providing common ground for people from different political traditions.

The real divide as far as most people in something like the Koenji underground are concerned, is between the hegemonising swarm that is mainstream culture and what basically amounts to Everything Else. What that Everything Else actually consists of is less important than the fact of its existence: the fact of its otherness. And from this you actually start to find links and crossovers forming between all kinds of things that wouldn't normally be considered natural bedfellows, but which have in each other found themselves "brothers in subculture".

SUBCULTURE AND IDOL MUSIC

It's a sold-out show and members of the crowd are headbanging furiously, sweat rainbows arcing from their hair as they pound and mosh to the beat. On the stage there is no band, just six girls in colour-coded costumes performing a cover of the Beastie Boys' Sabotage *to a backing track.*

Later on in the set, the girls take a break from the music to do a series of tear-streaked theatrical monologues. They were sad, but now they are happy. They are happy because of their fans. Thank you, fans: we couldn't do this without you. Some of the fans wipe tears from their eyes. We support you, Dempagumi Inc, we love you!

The music comes back on. The crowd goes wild again.

Japanese music over the past fifteen years has been a story of two parallel, often overlapping narratives. One is of a mainstream that's honed its message down to almost nothing, pushing alternative ideas out in its search for perfect homogeneity. The other narrative is one of alternatives that have continued to exist, and in some cases thrive, in a fragmented, balkanised state. The culture of fragmentation has been particularly strong in Tokyo and the search for ways to cross or transcend those divisions has occupied the thoughts and activities of many of the capital's

188

greatest musical minds.

One force that unites the fragmented alternative scenes in Tokyo is the idea of "subculture", which in Japan generally refers to cultural artifacts that exist outside the accepted mainstream and are looked down upon as crass or exploitative. Japanese subculture encompasses kung fu, pro-wrestling, various sorts of live comedy, bondage art, animation, horror films, punk rock and new wave. Subculture can be anything that's a bit trashy or that occupies a similar position outside the mainstream.

Idol music in its current form is still a subcultural artefact, despite having risen to being the dominant musical form of 21st Century Japan and having almost singlehandedly propped up the nation's music sales at a time of near unbroken decline.

The idols of the 70s and the 80s, sure, they were part of mainstream pop culture, but that died in the 90s, killed off by Tetsuya Komuro when he swiped the eternal Seiko Matsuda's crown and invented J-Pop. Idols were an underground phenomenon through the 90s, kept alive by otaku as an adjunct to anime and manga fandom. A brilliant and chilling depiction of the state of the idol scene in the 90s is director Satoshi Kon's animated masterpiece *Perfect Blue*. The small, cheaply produced concerts to sparse crowds of pretty much exclusively male outsider fans, the main character's cramped living conditions on an unfashionable railway line, and the popping champagne corks when an idol group cracks the lower reaches of the Top 100 with their new single. The idol lifestyle depicted in *Perfect Blue* is something that most indie bands would find familiar in many ways.

The big difference is in management. An idol was an employee of a talent agency who paid them a salary, something not unknown for indie bands, but very rare. So idol music's fan culture became decidedly non-mainstream, but its management remained commercial. With this in mind, it's worth paying close attention to the business model behind the idol scene.

The idol revival kicked off right at the tail end of the 90s with Morning Musume's hit *Love Machine*. The group's producer, Tsunku, was a rock musician himself with the band Sharam Q, but his approach to idol production was essentially nostalgic. The group emerged from a TV audition * and followed the interchangeable "mass idol" format that Onyanko Club had pioneered in the 80s. The whole thing was pitched as a kind of music family rather than simply a business, with "shuffle groups" of members and solo stars appearing together for one-off special singles acts as a way of cross-promoting different projects and reinforcing brand identity. Morning Musume and their sister projects were exercises in looking back at the golden age of idol music as mainstream culture, but subcultural consumption patterns had nevertheless begun to define them. The element of interchangeability that Tsunku played up had particular appeal to the database-like mindset of anime/manga otaku, and the wealth of side projects appealed to the collector's mentality of subculture enthusiasts.

The male counterpart to the female idol world is dominated

---

* Strictly speaking the audition was to find a singer for Tsunku's band and the future Morning Musume members were runners up later corralled into their own group.

190

by the Johnny & Associates talent agency, which since the 1960s has gradually clawed together a near-monopoly of male idols developing through groups like Four Leaves, Hikaru Genji, SMAP, Arashi, and more recently SexyZone and Kis-My-Ft2. While Johnny & Associates, under the control of its ageing proprietor Johnny Kitagawa, has a rather old fashioned, top-down management structure and is a far more established part of the mainstream than its female counterparts, it nonetheless promotes its acts by reinforcing the brand identity of the agency with a network of subgroups and trainees.

This network model of Japanese boy bands and idol groups shares a lot in common with the way foreign indie labels often operate. Indie labelmates tour together, fill in for each other – due to sickness or overindulgence – and they produce as well as make guest appearances on each others' work. You can see this in a lot of classic 80s UK labels of the punk and postpunk era like Stiff, Mute, Él, Factory, Sarah etc. It also strongly echoes the way the new wave Nagomu label gathered its own distinctive fanbase, built around the brand of the label itself.

However, the commercial Great Leap Forward that the business model took was in 2005 when Onyanko Club producer Yasushi Akimoto returned to his old idol stomping grounds by starting AKB48.

The group's slogan, "The idols you can meet", was designed to foster a sense of closeness with fans. This artificial intimacy was reinforced by nightly performances in the small theatre Akimoto had built for AKB48 in the otaku shopping district of Akihabara, from where the group also took their name. While earlier idol revivalists like Tsunku were nostalgic for the bright 80s, Akimoto's new venture looked to idol culture's dark days of the 90s. With their manufactured intimacy, AKB48 become one of the biggest pop phenomena in recent Japanese music history, but their appeal was built on the foundation of a small club environment that privileged close contact between performers and fans.

Akimoto's major achievement was in how, having fostered a sense of intimacy between idols and fans, he then managed to monetise it so effectively. The small size of the AKB48 theatre meant that it was constantly oversubscribed, so fans had to apply for tickets by lottery. Want to qualify for the lottery? Then buy their stuff. Want to meet the girls and touch them? Then buy more of their stuff and you can shake their hands. Want to get involved in the group's management by promoting the careers of the girls you like best? Why, you can simply vote for the members you want to see dancing at the front at concerts or appearing in the videos: one copy of the new single gives you one vote, but buy a hundred or a thousand and you can vote again and again!

This capitalistic form of idol-democracy plays off a distinctly non-mainstream fan mindset. The small, intimate spaces and the close contact with performers is obviously a key feature of the indie and underground music scenes. The fan involvement in the group's internal management is rather different, however, with closer parallels in the gaming world. For example in the Japanese game genre of "princess management simulators", players would take on the role of a father figure who guides a young girl through life into adulthood. Idol groups often encourage a similarly paternalistic relationship between fans and singers, with fans encouraged to see their role as supporting the hopes and dreams of one or more girls in the group. More explicitly lewdly, "dating simulator" games and various sorts of "visual novels" present a large cast of girls, one of whom the player will end up getting together with as a result of the in-game choices he makes. While console versions tend to include less in the way of bodily fluids than PC versions, these stories tend to make a big deal out of the idea of destiny, and even in their pornographic incarnations the version of love they present is often a self-consciously pure-hearted one, underscored by a sort of voyeuristic fetishism. The player and the girl are destined to be together, and yet paradoxically the player is encouraged to play the game multiple times in order to have a go on each girl's story. AKB48 is in many ways like a massively multiplayer live version of one of these games. The songs constantly urging fans to grasp for a chance of a romantic encounter, yet access to the objects of desire is strictly circumscribed and devotion to the group is instead measured exclusively by the amount of money spent. The result of this investment ends up looking increasingly like a late-capitalist pastiche of the true love AKB48 preaches.

Because of the huge amounts of money that both Akimoto's organisation and the fans themselves have invested in this illusion of intimacy, the maintenance of that illusion becomes of paramount importance. For example, no matter how commercially successful the idols may become, they must always be seen to be struggling – preferably with a camera nearby to record the tears. It's a system that fosters the idea that the fans are an essential part of the support network that allows the girls to achieve their dreams, which then act as a vicarious substitute for the fans' own dreams. The "dream" of the idols is an abstract thing though, and all it really amounts to is the circular logic of pleasing the fans – after all, what is the purpose of an idol other than to be idolised? What it comes down to is that while AKB48 fans are encouraged to believe they are supporting the girls' dreams, what they're really doing is defining those dreams as pleasing the fans – essentially asserting ownership over them.

PUPPETS OF SAWDUST, PUPPETS OF SOUND:

A girl looks into the camera and apologises. She was foolish to have violated our trust. She bows in supplication. Tears are in her eyes. Her hair has been completely shaved off. She insists that she did this herself as a gesture of penance. She apologises again for being such a poor role model, for disappointing her fans. She begs them for forgiveness. She was stupid and deserves punishment. She doesn't know why she did what she did. She is ashamed. Humbly, most humbly, she leaves her future in the hands of the men who support her and the men who manage her.

Fans and media outlets discuss this matter seriously. What the girl did was certainly wrong, but she has shown a sincere desire to repent. Yes, she is only human and we must forgive her. Of course she must be punished, but not too harshly. We will allow her a path back into our hearts.

Her crime had been having a boyfriend.

No-dating clauses in contracts have become a notorious symbol of the relationship between idols and fans. Similar rules apply in many boy bands, where fans can be every bit as fanatical and possessive, although the rules are not as strictly enforced with men. One reason for this is surely that female idols are far more vulnerable to the stalkerish attentions of obsessive fans, although the clauses usually go far further than fan interactions and cover relationships with anyone. Needless to say the burden of punishment is always placed squarely and publicly on the girl herself. The most notorious case of idol shaming was early in 2013, when AKB48's Minami Minegishi shaved her head and appeared on film sobbing and begging for forgiveness before being demoted by the group's management until she could learn to behave herself.

A lot of Minami Minegishi fans, both in Japan and abroad, made the argument that she had signed up for a no-boyfriend contract and thereby had no right to complain about punishments for breaking it. This is position is shortsighted at best and disingenuously swerves the point at worst. Minegishi signed that contract when she was a child, and while the contracts are renewed fairly regularly, once a childhood has been uprooted, aspiring idols are not in a position to ask for different treatment from their peers. She could be replaced immediately with one of the hundreds of other girls eager for the chance. The question is over the legitimacy of the rule in the first place, not whether AKB48 members are naive or stupid enough to sign up to it. It's a rule that forces girls to trade away their sexual agency in return for their careers, and this is something neither management nor fans have the right to demand.

One argument that gained some traction on social media was that this is simply a cultural misunderstanding. There is a Japanese tradition of cutting one's hair as a symbol of a new start – something often depicted in anime and drama, albeit in rather less drastic forms, and it has some religious associations with

Buddhism. On the other hand, in Europe especially, the shaving of women's hair as punishment for sexual indiscretions has a clear parallels with the way, during the later stages of the Second World War, many French and Dutch women had their hair publicly and forcibly shaved for the crime of having slept with German soldiers. There were also strong emotional echoes of the shaved heads of Jewish women in Nazi concentration camps. The different cultural associations here should be taken seriously, but the Minegishi incident clearly placed her sexual agency at the centre of the repentance ritual. In this context, the way in which the shaving of a woman's hair symbolically erases her femininity, and by association her agency as a woman, makes this a dramatic and disturbing incident wherever you're from. Or to put it another way, I'm not sure tradition is sufficient excuse for just being a horrible shit to someone.

In any case, there are signs that AKB48's management may have misplayed this one. Minegishi's apology ritual was so excessive and so shocking that people who had previously ignored the cultish creepiness of the group and their fans were forced to at least privately confront these aspects of them and their culture. The situation was probably not helped when soon after Minegishi's scandal spilled onto newspaper cover pages, weekly tabloid *Shukan Bunshun* photographed the AKB48 general manager Tomonobu Togasaki at a love hotel with a nineteen year-old girl. The married father of two's explanation when confronted with the accusation, "You're having an affair with a college girl," was that she was a prostitute so that didn't count as having an affair – which, to be fair, he probably felt addressed his indiscretion every bit as comprehensively as Minegishi's apology. The significance of this incident was probably fairly minimal in the overall scheme of things, but it certainly provided a helpful example of the behavioural double standards that exist between the young women and girls who perform in these groups and the middle-aged men who control them.

Nevertheless, AKB48's business model may have reached its natural ceiling in its current form. While sales, bulked up by hardcore fans blowing millions on multiple copies of the same CD, remain very high, the group's growth seemed to plateau around 2012 and general cultural interest has visibly declined – a process helped along its way by many ordinary people turning away in either disgust or aggressive disinterest after the Minegishi incident. The current rise of idol groups has gone hand in hand with the curious way in which an essentially conservative otaku base has come to exert a disproportionate influence on the development of online and consumer culture. Future expansion of the AKB business model therefore depends on the extent to which mainstream consumers can be convinced to adopt otaku consumption patterns, as well as the extent to which the culture and values idols embody can accommodate themselves with the mainstream.

While otaku interests do more than others to shape idol fan culture, otaku are far from the only players. There are also what we might call *bonkura* guys – again, it's pretty much always guys – who cross over with otaku but have wider tastes in cult movies, pro wrestling and pretty much any other kind of trash culture. *Bonkura* basically formed the core fanbase of the idol group

Momoiro Clover Z, and their presence helps to explain why the quintet's image is less sexualised than AKB48: as the writer Patrick Macias beautifully summarised on his blog *An Eternal Thought in the Mind of Godzilla*, "To put it bluntly, a *bonkura* guy would prefer to jerk off to actual pornography." This also helped shape Momoiro Clover Z into something far less creepy and made the anarchic energy of their performances far more natural-seeming. Add in producers and songwriters like Kenichi "Hyadain" Maeyamada with his background in Shibuya-*kei* and Narasaki from metal/shoegaze/thrash band Coaltar of the Deepers and you have an idol group primed not just for mainstream crossover but tailor-made for indie subculture freaks.

The breakout idol success of 2012-14 was metal-themed idol trio Babymetal, who were also closely associated with Narasaki. One of the main subculture markets Babymetal courted was metal fans and they bolstered their credentials by recruiting musicians from the same rock and metal hinterlands they were courting. Babymetal also benefit from a strong influence of visual-*kei*, which is perhaps natural when you take something as heavy and loud as metal and marry it with something as camp and theatrical as idol music. Courting fans of metal and alluding to visual-*kei* therefore helped Babymetal establish a commercial niche despite a saturated domestic idol market. Thanks to the lingering overseas popularity of visual-*kei* and the overall silliness of the concept, it surely also helped them reach out to overseas audiences.

There's a telling moment on Babymetal's *My First Heavy Metal in Tokyo 2012* video where the English on-screen text asks the question, "What's going on in Japan?" A seemingly innocent piece of hype at first glance, there's also an awareness on display here of an alien gaze looking in, which suggests the people behind the group are on one level conscious of the oddness of what they're doing, and at the same time aware of the "weird Japan" media narrative that exists overseas. The willingness of the Western media to play along with this narrative in Babymetal's subsequent viral success is testament to both the cleverness of the group's Japanese producers and the laziness of the West in how it reports on Japan.

Domestic Japanese indie fans have also been supporting acts that cultivate images which challenge the AKB48-dominated idol format. Examples of such groups include Dempa Gumi inc., Negicco and BiS. These groups and others have eagerly courted indie, punk, metal and other subculture audiences with songwriters, cover versions, producers and collaborators drawn from sources as diverse as Kenji Ozawa of Shibuya-*kei* pioneers Flipper's Guitar, Pizzicato Five's Yasuharu Konishi, The Beastie Boys, London-based Japanese heavy psychedelic rockers Bo Ningen, Dr. Usui of neo-new wave/technopop unit Motocompo, and first generation Kansai noise terrorists Hijokaidan.

Idol music has also sprung up around specific subcultural scenes. Pastel-coloured pop duo Vanilla Beans are pure Shibuya-*kei*, Aira Mitsuki was conceived as a technopop idol in the mould of early Perfume, and Necronomidol draw on pop cultural touchstones around punk, hardcore and goth. Additionally, there are dozens of small-town idol groups of varying degrees of obscurity who act as cheerleaders for their own local areas, from

Southern Cross in Kagoshima to Snow*Drop in Sapporo. Some of these idol groups have taken indie band-like career trajectories and an increasing number of them are self-producing with creative control of their own music.

Despite the more egalitarian application of talent that some idol groups employ behind the scenes, however, most of the girls are still treated as dancing dolls recruited by management through auditions, often at a very young age. Others are trained and produced by stage school boot camps like the Hiroshima Actors' School or Sakura Gakuin and sold on to management companies and labels for profit. When children are separated out from society and trained for the specific purpose of being idols in a world where other idols and idol wannabees are their main peers, there's inevitably some exploitation involved on a management level. At the same time, pretty much all idol music encourages a sort of paternalistic relationship between fans and group members who "serve" them, which can have problematic implications too, especially when the girls are so young. Within the idol world all this occurs to varying degrees from group to group and management to management, but as long as this basic management and production model exists, it's not going to change radically. Nevertheless, the male-dominated idol production line is not the only route for young women into music.

THE PINK GUITAR

The sun shines down on the park. To one side of it there is a café with a line of tables in front. One of them is displaying small, individually wrapped cookies, each decorated with its own naive, rather childlike design. On another table, some postcards are arranged alongside homemade earrings and brooches, all sharing the same wilful and yet at the same time expertly balanced amateurishness in their aesthetic. A rack of clothes has been placed next to them – retro 50s-style dresses with floral patterns whose design identifies the fine line between refined and gaudy, and then pitches itself just a little over that line. Everything is very girly. Obsessively so.

Into the small park now, and the circus is in town. A woman dressed as a clown is performing a mime act with a series of hoops in front of some children, while jugglers and stilt walkers patrol the streets. There are more stalls set up, lining the edges of the park. You can buy clothes and accessories here too, although of a slightly different nature. Almost everyone, from the clown to the cookie salespeople, is a musician of some kind, and their target audience is definitively female.

"Which one do you want?" a mother asks her daughter, pointing at some badges – again, they are all individually wrapped.

"That one," says the girl, pointing to Joey Ramone.

Next to the badges and t-shirts, three little girls are learning how to

*play guitar from one of the fathers. The oldest has an acoustic guitar, as she's
the only one with arms long enough to comfortably reach the strings. The
other two have miniature electric guitars with built-in amps, one red and one
pink. This is their own little rock camp, and here in this backstreet annex of
the circus they've just formed their first punk band.*

From The Sex Pistols covering The Monkees to Dempagumi Inc.
covering Beastie Boys, a musical fascination has long existed
between punk and bubblegum extremes, and the two share a lot
in terms of simple thrills and disposable amateurishness.
Aesthetically, punk and bubblegum blend into each other even
more easily now, as technology puts pop-like production tools in
the hands of DIY musicians, and less tribal listening tastes allow
genres to mingle more freely.

They're still different though, and that little pink guitar
embodies the competing strains of musical influence that
surround girls in Japan, from the cutesy pastel world of idol pop
to the raw DIY culture of punk.

The difference between idol pop and the indie/underground
scene might seem obvious on the surface. However, there are
nonetheless many cases where the boundary between being an
idol and being an indie artist appropriating the imagery of idol
music are blurred, with some idols producing and writing for
themselves, and many playing gigs at underground venues. This
ambiguity reveals a growing grey area between not only indie and
idol fan culture, which has a large amount of crossover already,
but also indie and idol musician culture.

There's a precedent for this in the career of 1980s singer Jun

Togawa, who appropriated the trappings of idol singers of her era and used that starting point to deconstruct media representations of women and girls. But while Togawa had a point she was trying to make – in particular satirising the insipid romantic narratives of 80s pop and critiquing contemporary gender roles – idol-like elements are increasingly becoming no more than an aesthetic option or a marketing tool.

Tower Records was one of the first organisations to recognise that the boom in idol music could have implications for the promotion of indie artists as well. Tower already had experience promoting more conventionally idol-like music through its own T-Palette label, but the company also began putting on live showcases that threw together packages of tangentially musically-related acts simply by virtue of them having female singers. In a music scene that had been dominated by the dour, cynical rock of bands like Number Girl and their followers for the past decade, this focus on pretty, female singers felt new.

This was followed by a flurry of media interest in a musically dubious psuedo-genre of "girls bands" in 2013, via features in girls' fashion magazines *Spur* and *Nylon*. Lumping together the bubblegum new wave of Merpeoples, the Showa era retro rock of Kinoko Hotel and the avant-garde disco-noise of Nisennenmondai, the magazines focused in on the bands' core female members primarily as aspirational icons for the benefit of a female readership. None of these acts had anything really to do with idol music as a genre, but by gathering them together under a "girls" banner, whether for a male audience, as with idols, or a female one, as with fashion magazines, a similar sacrifice is still necessarily being made: music is made subservient to gender for the purposes of marketing.

While fashion magazines and corporate advertising agencies may be focusing on female artists for primarily commercial purposes, it's not necessarily an entirely negative thing. The diverse range of female artists in the *Spur* and *Nylon* features may not make much sense musically, but in making the music lifestyle appear attractive to their readers, it may have helped encourage some girls to join bands. Japan doesn't do too badly when it comes to female participation in the music scene, but guys are still a clear majority. This can make it intimidating for young girls to take a first step into the music world, and perhaps partly as a response to this, there are also self-produced all-female rock bands who package their own events along gender lines. Some all-female rock bands adopt a position of riot grrrl-influenced female solidarity, while others position themselves into the idol-styled, male gaze-orientated "cute girls" mode of promotion. Some underground organisers, either consciously or not, adopt elements of both approaches, attempting to reconcile cuteness and DIY/punk sensibilities in constructing their notion of femininity in music. Whatever the approach, having women directing things behind the scenes changes the meaning of what happens onstage, even when draped in the cutesiest of imagery.

Independent, female-orientated pop (sub)culture has had a complex relationship with aesthetic notions of prettiness and cuteness. Some of the most unapologetically feminist Japanese punks made their first fanzines in the 80s by cutting out and rearranging pictures from magazines like cute fashion bible *Olive Magazine*. A generation of female musicians grew up watching the pretty fighters of *Sailor Moon* save the day on a weekly basis in the early 90s. Exaggeratedly cute imagery is part of the fabric of life for girls growing up.

One place you can see a combination of extreme, feminised cuteness and DIY fundamentalism without any apparent compromise on either side is The Twee Grrrls Club DJ team, centred around scene queen Sumire Taya of the boutique and record store Violet & Claire. Taya is rooted in a very Western-influenced indiepop, lo-fi punk and fanzine culture, with roots about as far away from the idol scene as it's possible to get. However, the extent to which the Twee Grrrls fetishise the cute and pretty goes way beyond anything someone growing up in the UK or US in the 80s and 90s would recognise, manifesting itself most strongly in the home made crafts and accessories the collective's various members sell.

Taya told me in an interview that her promotion of female-focused indie culture centres on her love for the aesthetics and attitude. "I think girls are very fearless in good way – sometimes it's a little dangerous," she says, "They'll start some new thing or project without thinking it through. This impulsiveness is what gives birth to the kind of interesting girls' culture that I love."

Nevertheless, Taya is clear that there is a distinction between what she does and the riot grrrl movement from which she takes some of her key influences.

"My idea of riot grrrl is perhaps a bit different from the way it's generally understood", says Taya, "People always think something related to riot grrrl will be 'Feminist'. I don't think we [Twee Grrrls Club] are feminist, but we do love the culture that was raised by the 90s riot grrrl movement – Bikini Kill, Sleater Kinney so on. That was the starting point of independent girls' music culture."

Some might argue that if "independent girls' culture" isn't feminist, then what does the word actually mean? The Chicks' Riot event, organised by *Vamp* magazine proprietor Ayumi Tsubouchi, has similar riot grrrl roots with more of a Ramones/Joan Jett trash punk sensibility, but as with the Twee Grrrls, Chicks' Riot events also prominently feature delicately crafted and absurdly cute home made cookies and other products.

Entering the music scene via artist management and the male-dominated world of music journalism in the early 90s, Tsubouchi had to fight tooth and nail to be taken seriously, and perhaps as a result of those fights has far less hesitation in describing herself as a feminist. Nevertheless, she believes it would be difficult to make the direct approach of riot grrrl work in a Japanese context.

"I went to the first Ladyfest in Olympia, Washington in 2000," Tsubouchi says, "It was organised by the original riot grrrls, and I realised I needed to do something like this in Japan. At the same time though, I didn't want to just copy it completely. Ladyfest was explicitly political, but that approach doesn't transfer easily to Japan: those things – music, politics, culture – they don't coexist in the same sphere in Japan."

This is a point backed up by Aiha Higurashi of garage-punk/alt-rock band Seagull Screaming Kiss Her Kiss Her, whose struggle to make headway in the Japanese rock scene of the early 90s paralleled Tsubouchi's experience in journalism.

"Japanese women really care about the 'extremeness' of feminism," says Higurashi. "Sometimes I think of myself as a feminist and sometimes not. I like some parts of the thinking of feminism, but I don't want to think only one way. It's dangerous. Sometimes I need feminism – that's why I fought with so many men: because there was a bias I needed to fight against."

That perceived extremeness forms a barrier to the dissemination of any overt message. Instead, Tsubouchi's approach was to work on normalising the idea of women taking ownership of their own culture by simply doing it and leading by example.

Tsubouchi identifies the key fault line as lying not in the realm of aesthetics so much as the relationship between creativity and control.

"In the 90s I used to be the manager of an idol singer," explains Tsubouchi. "She never talked about music – guys would just give the music to her. She learned the songs, took singing lessons, practiced over and over, went on stage, on TV, into the studio, did commercials. She worked hard, but she was always following someone else's instructions."

Leaving that industry and taking the indie/DIY route, Tsubouchi came face-to-face with idol culture again when she had a child of her own.

"I once asked Melissa Logan of Chicks on Speed in an interview, 'What is a feminist?' and she said, 'feminist means creative'. My daughter is seven now and she's recently started saying, 'I want to be an idol'. I want to support her, but I say, 'You can do that, but you have to make your own music. I bought her a pink guitar and a little organ. I want her to be creative."

That pink guitar and little organ stand as a metaphor for many of the most successful expressions of "girls' culture" in the Japanese music scene, combining the cute, the childlike and the amateurish with a punkishly unpolished creativity. Whether you call it feminism or not, reconciling that combination of cutesy naïvety and raw creativity is key to understanding an important part of the relationship that exists in Japan between girls* and the music scene.

We should be wary of attributing this emphasis on cuteness to some archaic cliché of the submissive Oriental flower of Japanese femininity: anyone who has met the likes of Taya or Tsubouchi for even a moment would call that out as the reductive nonsense it truly is; they are both sharp, intelligent, tough-minded individuals. Still, it's hard to question that cuteness and prettiness as feminine virtues are more pronounced in the Japanese indie scene than they typically are in the West – indeed, the limits to which the Japanese indie scene pushes its combination of cuteness with self-produced DIY aesthetics is part of its appeal to many fans, of all genders, from overseas.

In some ways, this intersection of cuteness and creativity is also a function of the filtering through of capitalist behaviour

---

* While this kind of girly culture is not restricted in any way to girls by age, "girlishness" in a more abstract sense is an important part of it and we shouldn't be shy of the word.

into the indie scene, with it becoming less politically conscious and more lifestyle-orientated. The fetishisation of design is by no means a uniquely Japanese phenomenon, while the shift from music as the primary product musicians sell, towards goods and branded products has gone hand-in-hand with the decline in music sales everywhere.

However, it would be foolish and narrowminded of us to mock the pink guitar. Rather, I prefer to look at it from a positive perspective. What links the work of self-produced idol groups, indiepop collectives like Twee Grrrls Club, and more explicitly feminist projects like Chicks Riot is that they are women asserting some degree of ownership over "girls' culture". They may sometimes project an image of pastel-candy-flowerpetal-sugar-cinnamon-sweetness, but girls in Japan have grown up surrounded by hyper-cute imagery. To put it in Marxist terms, they have seized control of the means of production, and within indie music's informal economy, the culture they produce is now being circulated on more or less their own terms. In this sense, they aren't victims of imposed notions of cuteness and girlishness, but rather they are using them as creative tools, drawn from the broad palette of pop culture, and applying them to ends as diverse as the music scene itself.

SAY ANYTHING, SAY NOTHING

I get to the venue in the late afternoon. I'm just in time to see a ferocious no wave band called Otori, a band so tightly wired, so rhythmically taut, so face-meltingly intense that they render all other music in their immediate vicinity unnecessary. This show's going on for another six hours though, and it has a lot lined up.

Just down the hall, there's another stage, and navigating a chicane of girls holding timetables, one in a skintight silver jumpsuit, one with a ball gag worn coyly round her neck, I get to see the intricate, piano-based progressive rock of Hanazono Distance. This is immediately followed by the earsplitting fusillade of gnarled guitars and explosive drums of post-hardcore duo Bumbums. "Thank you!" the vocalist squeaks, grudgingly.

Back on another stage, seven girls in school uniforms with black feather wings attached are performing a sort of bubblegum-gothic song-and-dance. They're called Bell Ring Girls Heart (in Japanese: Bellring Shojo Heart) and they move and sound exactly the same as nearly all other idol music. They're tremendously enthusiastic, though, so who cares? What next? Tortured, emotionally-wrought grunge rock? A squeaky-voiced woman in a giant dog costume? Sure, we've got that and more.

What links all these acts, and indeed what the event is sold on, is the foregrounding of female artists, even if the images and ideals they present seem

211

in places mutually contradictory. That's just part of the book though: what
really pulls these disparate elements together is their relationship to subculture.

The broad church of subculture in Tokyo happily accommodates riot grrrl and idol influences under one roof. The female qualities are not on their own enough to give such an event meaning though: what matters more is that all the bands feel subcultural. Regardless of gender, if an organiser throws an eclectic and esoteric enough variety of lurid and loud things into a bowl together, they can have a subculture event. The key in this instance is to push the extremes of taste in all directions, while simultaneously marketing them under a unified theme. You want cute? Get the most exaggeratedly cute thing you can find. You want punk? Get the loudest, fastest punk with the craziest hair and most cartoonishly over-the-top stage manner you can find. You want girls? Stick them in cosplay and fetish outfits and have them walking around handing out cocktails – as long as everything's done with shameless theatricality and crass, gaudy bad taste, you're probably working along the right lines. Two completely mutually contradictory messages can be placed side-by-side in a Japanese subculture event and it doesn't matter, because the manner of their expression is what counts more than the content.

To see how subcultural positioning and its mode of expression work, a good example is to look at idol music from the perspective of an underground music fan.

As this book has already discussed, modern idol music is fundamentally a subcultural artefact, and has forged various connections with the underground. In a subcultural environment, idol groups are welcome alongside yowling, tortured grunge bands or screaming, sweating and bleeding punk rockers, not to mention pole dancers, porn star DJs, physical comedians, bondage artists, cosplay parades and this and that and the other and its grandma. The mix-and-match policy of this cultural environment is present within a lot of idol music itself, where a producer like Kenichi "Hyadain" Maeyamada can overlay melodies, rhythms, arrangements and genres to create music that is at once exuberant, giddily innocent and a tasteless, mangled car crash pop pileup. It's an appeal that recalls the dizzying sensory overload of being a child, experiencing the world in wild, fragmented laser-bursts of colour. The underground popularity of Maeyamada-produced acts like Momoiro Clover Z and Dempagumi Inc. came in large part because the groups' managers understood the appeal of this incoherent, high-octane, geek-trash, paint-splatter approach to pop culture.

Idol music's appeal as an alternative to the old J-Pop mainstream is also visible in the attitude towards beauty it often promotes. In the purest underground and otaku traditions, an idol need not be, and in many ways *should* not be, a conventional beauty. Her imperfections, her amateurishness, her physical plainness, her essential *normality* are the building blocks of the idol's character. An idol acts out a hero's journey of an ordinary schmuck with no great attributes except a dream and a burning passion to realise it. They encounter obstacles, they overcome them, and they fight their way through to the next small victory. It is a metaphorical narrative for the fan's understanding of their own life and the narrative doesn't work if all the girls are stunningly beautiful: the whole point of the dream is that it's democratic and should be available to any girl, and vicariously by any fan with the money to buy all the singles, drama CDs and branded products. Dempagumi Inc. are a case in point here, with a backstory that paints the group as former social shut-ins who overcame their difficulties and followed their dreams into a bright future. The girls themselves are not strictly — or at least not *only* — fetish objects of male sexual desire; they are avatars and objects of identification, acting out the central drama of the age: the struggle between the bleak reality of adult life and the glittering dreams of a childhood that is increasingly, perhaps infinitely prolonged by infantilising consumer culture. It may be heavily commercialised, but the message makes an explicit appeal to audience sensibilities that reject mainstream cultural life.

However, despite the anti-mainstream sensibility, commercialism is an inescapable part of both idol music and the subcultural mode of consumption. The dreams idol music promotes are directly hitched to a consumer culture where the only goal is the endless recycling and rehashing of the same basic products, packaging them as dreams, and then selling them back to the fans/consumers. In the end, everything is reduced to variations on the standard mainstream marketing format of pretty faces, comedy and nostalgia. We may criticise major labels and talent agencies for their reliance on those key elements, but those same three things are also at the core of the subculture model of music promotion.

Subculture-themed events often takes the simple, direct

pleasure and passion of punk, and draws parallels with the fetishised femininity of idols or nostalgic appeals to childhood ephemera. The appeal of all these things is in being something raw, unvarnished, and untouched by the adult world. In order to make this parallel, though, you need to adopt a very simplified view of punk or indie music that focuses only on its most infantile virtues – the energy, the "kids-wanna-have-fun" attitude, the temporary rejection of the adult world – and de-emphasise the more controversial elements. Essentially, subculture smooths over the differences between distinct genres by seeking the lowest common denominator.

The trade-off that such a crossover offers is that punk and alternative musicians give idols credibility and buzz that can serve as a stepping stone to real success, while idol music offers indie artists access to a slightly bigger audience. This marketing model may be crass but it's effective in bringing crowds to events. Moreover, fluidity between these different scenes provides economic opportunities for musicians from alternative backgrounds to get a foot in the idol-industrial-complex as professional songwriters or producers. But when indie and punk are treated by organisers and consumed by audiences in the same way as idol music, they lose some of their meaning, becoming just a few more elements in a shop display of kitsch. In this way, mainstream culture and subculture are more similar than they at first seem. Mainstream culture burns different voices away to create a homogeneous whole devoid of meaning; meanwhile, the subculture aesthetic throws together so many different sets of contradictory messages that it drowns out the messages' content in cultural noise. In this sense, subculture is not a true alternative to the mainstream, but rather a method – with no particular values of its own – of marketing the *sensation* of being alternative. Subculture has immense value in pulling together disparate genres and ideas in often giddily exciting ways, but it also suffers from some of the mainstream's same inherent trends towards the superficial.

IN THE END, THOUGH...

Japanese subculture has grown into a recognisable market sector. This transformation is part of a broader trend, and not necessarily a completely negative one. Despite its increasing commodification, Japanese subculture contains within it a refusal to identify with any specific tribe or market demographic.

I am hopeful that audiences and musicians will continue to care less for the strict and precious genre discrimination that has segregated music so much in Tokyo. In a way, any increasing diversity of lineups and collaborations in the Japanese capital would simply mean that Tokyo was becoming more like the rest of the country, where the local live circuit is too small to accommodate much genre snobbery. Nevertheless, because of its dominant position in the Japanese music world, changes in Tokyo's attitudes are still of great significance in the music scene nationwide.

The mainstream has consolidated around music that is so featureless, empty and remote that it has left a vacuum beneath. Idol and anime music have a strong formative influence on musicians as they grow up, and perhaps more importantly, they currently provide a route between the underground and mainstream. That route is narrow though, and as the music industry shrinks (or musicians themselves become a less important part of it), it's going to get narrower. The void the mainstream has left, however, is only going to grow, and that brings with it incredible freedom and almost endless possibilities. The willingness to exploit those possibilities will be the test of the indie and underground scenes' strengths. Musicians and fans may increasingly refuse to identify with political or scene-political affiliations, but a refusal to *identify* doesn't have to mean a refusal to *do*.

For Japanese indie artists who don't opt to write for idol groups, the music scene is fraught with financial and institutional problems. Artists must bear the costs of playing live, touring and recording, the lack of label and distribution support, the difficulty of disseminating information and a major label death-lock on traditional media infrastructure. But while many in the Tokyo underground scenes and even the major labels have been pessimistic about the future, there has been over the past ten years a growing awareness of and motivation to deal with the situation. The generation of musicians coming through now have set up new institutions on an ad-hoc basis. Many young musicians are less willing to pay venues for the privilege of playing, learning instead from the punk scene to set up DIY shows in studios or more unorthodox venues. The new generation of musicians in Tokyo seems to value atmosphere over high-end PA setups. Musicians are making use of technology that allows them to record, release and distribute music theirselves with far greater ease than before. Even the broadening of idol culture and the commodification of subculture are part of this process of building an alternative, setting up a parallel indie economy.

I'm not going to pretend, like some Silicon Valley TED evangelist, that the economic hollowing out of the music business is any kind of glorious, disruptive financial opportunity. There's no point: the Japanese indie scene is already the Silicon Valley oligarchs' dream of a cash-for-access, work for love-not-money economy of willing slavery. But the openness and the potential for the breaking down of old segregations must at least be considered a great opportunity on a creative level, allowing artists to explode and reassemble music in new ways, outside the influence of strictly-defined genre scenes. With the mainstream so remote and the few routes to reach it so congested, there is little at stake for someone wanting to try something different or new. History suggests that while Japan's mainstream music industry tends to move in technologically- and industrially-driven fits and starts, the underground – from the suppressed and ostracised 1970s rock scene of Les Rallizes Dénudés to the current mishmash of noise, technopop, folk, electro, comedy and punk – has continued as it pleases, propelled by impulses far more resilient than money.

The story of alternative music in Japan can be naïve, grasping, egocentric, snobbish and vulnerable to the most ridiculous fads – often all at the same time – but what keeps it going is a devotion that defies all financial common sense. In the end, it's a story about love.

APPENDICES AND SCENE NOTES:

THE MUSICAL SOUNDTRACK OF THIS BOOK
AND WHERE IT CAME FROM

JAPANESE RECORD LABELS AND REGIONAL SCENES

There is so much going on in the Japanese indie scene that I have no access to or knowledge about, and it is all so constantly changing that providing a comprehensive, up-to-date guide to what's happening would be far beyond my ability. Nevertheless, what provided my musical foundations in the Japanese underground and which soundtracked my writing of this book, from early 2014 to late 2015, can be categorised loosely into music from scenes that I'll describe in detail on the next few pages.

OMOCHI RECORDS

The banner under which Shinnosuke Mochizuki of the venue Shinjuku Loft carries out his musical activities, Omochi Records encompassed two main regular or semi-regular events. One of these was Shin Juke. Ostensibly a dance-juke event but probably not in any form that someone from the juke's original city of Chicago would recognise, Shin Juke's emphasis was on DJs but it also incorporated live acts, especially those with electronic and hip hop influences. At Shin Juke, the brasher and more hysterically animated the better. Performers ranged from indie dance bands like Have a Nice Day! to food–obsessed hip hop duo Y.I.M. and DJ team LEF!!! Crew!!!. At the centre of it all was electro-nonsense collective Nature Danger Gang, whose onstage performances incorporated elements of cosplay, bondage, full male nudity and random violence with a fluid lineup of dancers, rappers and the occasional musicians. Nature Danger Gang were trashy, funny, occasionally sexy, sometimes an incomprehensible mess – and, unlike a lot of the more theatrical underground events, I often got a real sense that some of the performers might genuinely hurt themselves. The music was a relentless clatter of beats delivered with an irrepressible and joyous disregard for good taste.

Many Shin Juke acts cross over with Omochi's other event Scum Park. This featured a lineup that leaned more towards the punk and alternative scenes, albeit delivered with the same raucous enthusiasm. Noise punk maniacs Manga Shock, subculture dweeb-punks Guessband and funk-punk glamazons Fat Fox Fanclub were all bands who occasionally graced the stage here.

What links all of the acts at these events and what they represent more widely in the Tokyo underground scene is a trend towards militant and eclectic coudln't-give-a-fuckery: party politics in the most hedonistic sense of the word.

KANSAI UNDERGROUND

The Kansai scene is wide and varied, encompassing all kinds of acts from Kyoto, Osaka, Kobe and beyond. There is a strong underground tradition in the area as it was once a key breeding ground for Japan's nascent punk scene. Kansai was home to Inu, Ultra Bide and Aunt Sally, as well as the place where Japanese noise was born with acts like Hijokaidan, Incapacitants, Masonna, Hanatarash and more. Osaka bands like Boredoms and Shonen Knife were also pivotal in raising awareness of Japanese alternative music overseas.

In the mid-2000s, there was a sudden wave of domestic interest in Kansai bands, with a number of notable acts gaining a following in Tokyo under the banner of the *"Kansai Zero Sedai"* ("Kansai Zero Generation"). This phenomenon may have been partly manufactured by Tokyo organisers and venues, but it sent a powerful message to indie fans that underground rock didn't have to be gloomy and serious. Osaka's Afrirampo became stars—with their furiously nonsensical, ultra-lo-fi, semi-improvised, art-primitive garage-punk – and they were quickly snapped up by Sony, who sent them to America to record an album that sounded like someone frying chips in a tank battle.

Then came eclectic, parentheses-misusing Kyoto punk band Limited Express (Has Gone?); the hyperactive, colour-coded Ni-Hao!; Kyōjin Yueni Dekai, an avant-garde duo featuring a guy on stilts mutilating a guitar; the blood, sweat and vomit-soaked performance riot of Oshiripenpenz; and sub-Sabbath riff-merchants Watusi Zombie. At the tail end of the 2000s Kansai boom was Midori, a piano-led, jazz-influenced punk band whose singer wore a mixture of schoolgirl uniform and duct tape as she screeched at and clambered over the audiences. Midori were also put out by Sony and came within a hair's breadth of becoming genuinely mainstream stars – so say what you will about the majors, but every once in a while, something truly odd and unique makes it through.

What linked Kansai bands was a sense of performance that managed to be theatrical and often comical, but rarely goofy. It was a balance that Tokyo bands have often struggled to attain. In the capital, bands will frequently shed their cool to play the fool or become so wrapped up in themselves and their art that all the energy and fun is sucked from the performance. So when all these Kansai bands struck at once, there was an immediate sense of something different.

Nevertheless, such impressions of mine about the Kansai scene are informed by my Tokyo-centric eye, and Kansai is big enough to offer a wide range of diversity. While bands like Afrirampo set pulses racing, in 2004 the more low-key *No New Namba* compilation came out, featuring the atmospheric no wave of bands like Squimaoto and Passion, and some of the most enduring Kansai underground bands of the era are in this vein, such as the fiercely minimal Yolz in the Sky, the jittery new wave of BLONDnewHALF and the taut, wired postpunk of Fluid. Towns in the Kansai area continue to produce a staggeringly diverse range of music in a variety of genres, with eclectic Kyoto indiepop and dance music label Second Royal just one example of the broad musical range the area has to offer.

KYUSHU UNDERGROUND

Perhaps due to its remoteness from Tokyo, the city of Fukuoka on the island of Kyushu has often been a source of music that runs contrary to established trends in the capital, from the gasoline roar of *mentai* rock in the 1970s to the hybrid scene that gave us Number Girl in the 1990s. Hajime Yoshida of Panicsmile described Fukuoka to me as being a case of bands looking to Tokyo for what's cool, but due to a lack of information, getting it wrong in interesting ways. Makoto Ayukawa of *mentai* rock legends Sonhouse and Sheena & The Rokkets says that for his generation Tokyo was less relevant than London or New York as a source of influences.

A combination of the web and a boom in low cost air travel has brought Fukuoka and its deep hinterland closer to the rest of Japan in recent years. Increased contact with artists in the region has perhaps diminished the distinctive identity the area might have had. It may also be the case that greater ease of access to music in Fukuoka has revealed how Tokyoites' fantasies of the place were romanticised, and it offers the same broad variety of music as elsewhere.

Through my own work with the magnificent postpunk band

Hyacca, Fukuoka has become a sort of home-away-from-home for me. My first visit there was a key event in motivating me to start my label in earnest, and it's clear that while Kyushu lacks the fashionable, internationalised side of indie culture that Tokyo and to a lesser extent Nagoya and Kyoto have in abundance, bands there nevertheless mine a rich seam of intelligent, imaginative alt-rock that manages to be cool without being overtly fashion-conscious.

Hyacca guitarist Hiromi Kajiwara is notable also for her work with sophisticated synth-led new wave/avant-pop trio Miu Mau, while bassist Seiji Harajiri's management of the venue Utero has helped to act as a bridge between Fukuoka and the rest of Japan, a gateway to the rest of Kyushu, and a sort of alternative scene hub. Bands like Macmanaman, who play instrumental post-rock with the ferocity of a hardcore band, and funk-punk animals Accidents in Too Large Field represent the noisier side of Fukuoka. The city also plays host to the tropical prog pop of Nontroppo, the lo-fi avant-blues of Folk Enough and the lush indiepop of Hearsays.

Deeper into Kyushu, the city of Kumamoto has bands like Doit Science, who make thrillingly disorientating off-kilter alt-rock with a Beefheartian approach to song construction and a penchant for nonsensical multi-part harmonies. Nagasaki's Neue Sanssouci are a bewildering hotpot of raygun new wave, Cardiacs-style hyperactive prog-pop weirdness and chiptune hardcore – like a headache made of broken arcade machines. On the southern tip of Kyushu, the island Kagoshima gave me psychotic garage-punk eccentrics Zibanchinka, whose vocalist

Iguz Sōseki went on to form the heavy psychedelic collective Futtachi. In Saga, the frantic, hyperkinetic Hakuchi were mindblowing while the screaming teens of Nakigao Twintail gave this book its title, promptly followed their own advice and split up, and then re-emerged here in Tokyo just as I was working my way through final edits of this book.

NAGOYA UNDERGROUND

One of the good things about the city of Nagoya's alternative scene is the way a couple of strong record stores/labels have managed to hold on, providing a sort of hub for local music. Stiff Slack is the starting point for post rock and old-school emo sounds, while File-Under (and its associated Knew Noise label) is the place to go for more indie and new wave-influenced acts.

The 2012 Knew Noise compilation album *Ripple* is a terrific starting point for a lot of the best music from the city, featuring excellent tracks from bands like Freedom, Sekaitekinaband, Nicfit, Zymotics and more. Time and erosion have seen many of the featured bands fall by the wayside since, but the same people continue to crop up in superb new bands. The *7586 Nagoya Rock* compilation series is also a useful introduction to the diverse range of sounds the city offers. At the time of writing, 6Eyes remain a discombobulating mixture of sleazy lounge jazz and explosions of hardcore, Free City Noise are top notch Sonic Youth-influenced art-punks, Rock Hakaba are a thrilling psychedelic garage rock sleigh ride, Pop Office are solid melodic rockers, The Act We Act are Aichi Prefecture's shrieking masters of skronk, Crunch offer an elegantly crafted and melancholy brand of pop and The Moments hold down Nagoya's end of the jangly, C86-style indiesphere.

INDIEPOP

The indiepop scene in Japan is an interesting study in the evolution of language in pop. Having been a relatively recent import, via Trattoria Records and Shibuya-*kei* in the 1990s, it exists with one foot in the international world of imported European and American music and one in a scene of gradually developing Japanese stylistic translations. English and Japanese languages exist side by side, but the Japanese side seems to be gradually floating away into its own sphere while the English side continues to hang around by the door, listening for any sounds that might drift in from outside.

Shibuya-*kei* took indiepop as one of its starting points, and there are many bands in a loosely indiepop vein that share some DNA with Shibuya darlings Flipper's Guitar as well as Japan's own, older melodic pop-rock tradition. Whisper-voiced geek-popsters Soutaisei Riron, indie rock pretty boys Mitsume, and dreampop weavers Jesse Ruins all started out with loose sonic or scene affiliations to indiepop and Shibuya-*kei*, but each went on to become very much their own thing.

A good place to look for jangly new developments in indie when I was first finding my way through the Tokyo music scene was the Twee Grrrls Club DJ collective. Acting as deck-spinning guns for hire on multiple local events as well as hosting foreign bands on tour, they act as a sort of scuzzy, lo-fi bridge between Japan and the rest of the world. The delicate and ethereal She talks Silence first made an appearance via Twee Grrrl Sumire Taya's Violet & Claire label, while former Twee Yuppa (who records herself as Hazel Nuts Chocolate or more recently HNC) released the almost painfully authentic-sounding Smiths/Pale Fountains/Aztec Camera-influenced Sloppy Joe through her White Lily Records.

Fukuoka's Dead Funny Records burst onto the scene in 2012 and swiftly built up a solid catalogue of releases from bands like Fukuoka locals Hearsays, Tokyo's Boyish and Aomori shoe-gazers The Earth Earth. Their compilation *Dead Funny Compilation Vol.1* was something of a who's-who of chiming guitar-slingers and fuzzbox-abusers, featuring the energetic Half Sports, Nagoya's gentle Old Lacy Bed and harmony-laden Kyoto band Homecomings.

The home that Homecomings come home to, however, is Kyoto's Second Royal Records, who served as a kicking-off point for the scuzzy, Beach Boys-influenced indie romanticism of Teen Runnings. Nearby Osaka produced Wallflower, as well as the fragile, difficult-to-define and short-lived Jesus Weekend. Meanwhile, back in Tokyo, probably the best Japanese indiepop band of this generation is DYGL ("day-glo"), who eschewed the wispy, faintly disaffected coos and whispers of most of their Japanese contemporaries in favour of making something genuinely passionate and anthemic.

BAUHAUS/TOKYO NOISE

The two events named Bauhaus and Tokyo Noise don't so much
represent any kind of real, existing scene so much as a filter: a
way of looking at music with a particular new wave/no
wave/postpunk-influenced tint to one's indoor shades. While
distinct from the *Tokyo New Wave of New Wave '98* generation in
its greater emphasis on foreign new wave influences like XTC,
Gang of Four and the Contortions rather than Japanese ones like
P-Model and the Plastics, the organisers are not dogmatic about
strict adherence to a particular style. Of greater concern to them
is the exploratory spirit of the era they idolise.

The now seemingly defunct *Tokyo Noise* was organised by
members of the band You Got a Radio, a spiky postpunk band
combining elements of Gang of Four, XTC, Joy Division and
Magazine, while *Bauhaus* was founded by the band Dead Pan
Speakers, whose driving mixture of disco and motorik echoes the
functional lines of the original Bauhaus architectural movement
from which the event takes its name. There are close ties
between both events and the twin venues Three and Basement
Bar in Shimokitazawa, which have over the years been supportive
to bands that show an omnivorous but arty idiom.

Probably the best band to emerge from this general orbit has been Extruders. A trio who began as a sort of calmer version of UK postpunks Wire (and actually once played a set composed ent-irely of covers taken from Wire's 1978 masterpiece *Chairs Missing*), Extruders gradually evolved into a purveyor of delicate, borderline psychedelic musical soundscapes, where the spaces between sounds came to hold as much significance as the sounds themselves. Crossover with the Nagoya scene is evinced in how they regularly toured with the gothic/postpunk band Zymotics and released the magnificent album *Colors* through Nagoya's Knew Noise label.

Other bands you might have found at Bauhaus or Tokyo Noise events have included the relatively orthodox new wave band Keen Monkey Work, Cibo Matto-esque hip hop-influenced duo Y.I.M., thundering industrial/EBM duo Group A, new wave/avant-pop band Compact Club, junk/hardcore band Halbach and trancelike drum/guitar duo Kirihito, many of whom are fixtures in utterly unrelated scenes, but all of whose music and aesthetic sense contains some of the creative flavour of the late 70s and early 80s. As I say, it's a "scene" that doesn't really exist as a discrete entity, but it reveals how a broad knowledge of the indie music landscape, coupled with a keen eye for aesthetic tendencies and a bit of lateral thinking, can create something thematically coherent out of nothing, as well as how abstract many of the more established genre and scene boundaries are in the first place. Both events provided important encouragement to me in my stumbling ongoing attempts to do something similar.

TECHNOPOP/POST-SHIBUYA-KEI

The end of Shibuya-*kei* coincided with the brief appearance of a new generation of new wave and technopop-influenced bands. The *Tokyo New Wave of New Wave '98* compilation is something I've discussed earlier in this book, and its influence lingered long after the scene itself had ceased to be relevant. One of the places the remnants of Shibuya-*kei* and this revival of interest in technopop came together was on the Usagi-Chang label. The *Usagi-Chang Superstar!!* compilation featured *TNWONW98* band Motocompo and introduced the decidedly Shibuya-styled Aprils, as well as Eel, Macdonald Duck Eclair, Sonic Coaster Pop, Pine*am and the magical Plus-tech Squeeze Box. The label later helped introduce 8-bit chiptune jazz-pop unit YMCK, while the likes of Hazel Nuts Chocolate (basically the solo project of future Twee Grrrl Yuppa) and Capsule (future Perfume and Kyary Pamyu Pamyu producer Yasutaka Nakata's project) were also affiliated.

The success of Nakata's work with Perfume and the subsequent boost to Capsule's profile in the mid-2000s led to a mini-boom in idol-styled electropop with singers like Aira Mitsuki and Saori@Destiny (later Saoriiiii), and slick, synth-heavy pop duos like Sweet Vacation, usually featuring a female singer with an autotuned voice and some guy standing behind a Macbook. None of them never really hit the big time, but this evolution of Shibuya-*kei* and technopop eventually became accepted as a thing in its own right and coalesced around events like *Tokyo Eleport*. The irrepressibly joyful Candles were one of the best examples of this scene.

Despite my predilection for the raw and skronky, I have also been tangentially involved in some of the dissipated remains of technopop and Shibuya-*kei* via the event Switched On. This event began life conceived as a new wave party, and it evolved to incorporate remnants of the "new wave of new wave" in former Spoozy's keyboardist Rola Korpi's V/order, electropop newcomers like Candles, self-produced idol styled group Electric Ribbon and erotic subculture cabaret The Lady Spade (*Sono Na wa Spade* in Japanese). Motocompo themselves morphed into self-styled "ska-electro" faux boyband (M)otocompo (the "M" is silent). My own limited role tended to be to show up at Switched On events looking scruffy and haggard, torment the anime and idol music fans with discordant blasts of 1980s German industrial music and then retreat to the bar with a confused and slightly scared half-smile on my face for the rest of the evening. Switched On was a superb event and I'm ashamed of nothing.

TOKYO BOREDOM

My first real understanding of the alternative scene in Tokyo as a coherent, interconnected thing came through going to see bands at places like 20000V in Koenji, Motion in Shinjuku, Club Goodman in Akihabara and Em 7 (and later BushBash) in Koiwa. Draw a line through these places on a map and you have a neat line bisecting the city along the path of the Chuo and Sobu Lines. The term "Chuo Line music" isn't widely accepted, but at the same time it's a phrase that you can toss around and people familiar with underground music will quickly catch on to what you mean. The event that encapsulates it best is Tokyo Boredom.

While Tokyo Boredom has happened all over the city and as far afield as Kyoto and even Taipei, its musical roots lie in the venues 20000V and Club Goodman. Run by a collective of musicians, Tokyo Boredom started out as a free party and a gift to fans, swelling to a huge festival, and then went further afield. The key rule is that the organisers must never get bored, otherwise, ironically, Tokyo Boredom would lose all meaning and stop.

Core bands have over the years included funk-punk-dub band Bossston Cruizing Mania, metallic junk noise monstrosity

Groundcover, the rhythmically deranged but heart-stoppingly joyous Tacobonds, prog-garage-surf rockers Worst Taste, ex-Kyoto punk eccentrics Limited Express (Has Gone?), and jittery skronk maniacs The Mornings.

Crossing over slightly with Tokyo Bordem, events like the Minna no Senkan series are a bit more progressive and post-rock influenced, with bands like Henrytennis, Loolowningen & the Far East Idiots, the glorious psychedelic gypsy-punk trio Praha Depart and furious, totally wired and terrifyingly intense no wave quartet Otori. Back when they were based in Tokyo, Panicsmile were certainly part of the crowd that both the Boredom and Minna no Senkan events draw from. Many of these bands are affiliated with the label and distribution arms of independent record store chain Disk Union, while Panicsmile's own Headache Sounds label has drawn heavily from this pool of artists for its compilation albums in recent years.

Also crossing over with the Tokyo Boredom crowd has been the Less Than TV label. It has consistently operated very popular events and released a number of raucous, Boredom-related bands bands like Groundcover, Tiala and Limited Express. Put simply, Less Than TV is simply the best place in Japan to go for music that skirts the fringes of hardcore. Among some of the other fine bands to leave a mark on Less Than TV's roster are: Fukuoka's Accidents in Too Large Field, Osaka's Yolz in the Sky, Nagoya's Dancebeach, and the wonderfully camp yet hypnotically tight and laser-focused Deracine.

WHAT ELSE IS THERE?

A hell of a lot, is the short answer, and there isn't space either on these pages or indeed in my brain to do everything justice. I have tried to cover the music that had a strong impact on me as a music journalist, event organiser and label owner over the past ten years or so, and I am not ashamed to say that I have consciously skirted over a great deal of music that may be deemed significant but which I personally dislike, and used the platform the good people at Awai Books have offered me to shout loud from the rooftops about artists that I feel are worthy of greater acclaim (Don't like it? Write your own book). With that in mind, there is a lot of music that doesn't fit into any of these convenient pigeonholes that I have been working with up to this point, but which I feel deserves a shout-out.

Among bands I have worked with on my Call and Response are Hysteric Picnic, although they have changed their name to Burgh and are on a much better label now. They are a staggeringly talented band, taking a fistful of fashionable indie touchstones like Joy Division, Jesus And Mary Chain and The Birthday Party, crushing them into dust and transcending them in a way that their more reverential contemporaries always struggle

240

to achieve. Call and Response also released Synth-punk trio Jebiotto, who are a whirlwind of stadium rock melodies, torn to shreds in a drunken fury and set alight with a Molotov cocktail in a Jack Daniels bottle.

Uhnellys are special to me partly as being (until the success of Burgh) the only band I have ever released anything by to have gone on to become successful in any meaningful way. Basing their music around a series of delay loops created on guitar, bass, trumpet and vocals, they then add live drums and make the most thrilling jazz-, funk-, and garage rock-influenced hip hop imaginable.

Elsewhere in the Tokyo music scene, floating freely through any number of events and scenes on their sheer brilliance alone is the raw, brutal, pummelling kraut-noise of Kuruucrew, the electrifying minimal death disco of Nisennenmondai, the playground skronk of occasional-Twee-Grrrl-but-certainly-not-twee Moe Wadaka's Miila and The Geeks, and the many works of the obscenely talented Aiha Higurashi, of Loves, The Girl and Seagull Screaming Kiss her Kiss Her.

Japan has many other scenes, small and large, including a lively shoegaze scene led by bands like Lemon's Chair and Cruyff in the Bedroom and a suitably gloomy goth scene. Lively hardcore and industrial scenes remain, and the experimental descendents of 1970s and 80s pioneers like Hijokaidan, Ruins, Keiji Haino and others have never completely left my radar. The festivals put on by the magazine *Rockin' On Japan* promote a sort of soft-edged and mute-toned indie rock, which I usually find insufferably bland, but nevertheless still provides some opportunities for good bands. Similarly, organisers like Style Band Tokyo have also done a creditable if sometimes thankless job of introducing experimental, creative and raw music to audiences who would normally never have had the opportunity to encounter it. At the bottom of Tokyo's scene, it's easy to remain ideologically pure, but further up the ladder compromises become the rule, not the exception. That's why we must give credit wherever we see people up there helping genuine art find its place.

In line with this book's focus on my own subjective experiences I have talked briefly about the Nagoya, Kansai and Kyushu music scenes, but neglected entirely the Tohoku and Hokkaido areas of eastern Japan, the island of Shikoku and nearby Hiroshima, as well as almost the whole of the Sea of Japan coast. This is something I would dearly love to remedy in the future.

ACKNOWLEDGEMENTS

There are more people deserving of thanks than I could possibly credit here, but there are a few whose support has been invaluable over the past decade and more I've spent struggling at the bottom rung of the music scene.

Akiko, Atsushi and Tetsurō from The Students; Yoko and Kyōhei from Mir; Kajiwara, Goshima, Harajiri and Sasaki from Hyacca; Iguz Sōseki and all the Zibanchinkas and Futtachis; David Hickey and Sean McKenna at *The Japan Times*; James Hadfield, Ryōtarō Aoki, Shingo Nakagawa and all the Koenji/Call And Response crowd; everyone at 20000V; Rumiko and Isachan at Bamii; Matthew and everyone at Awai Books; Zana and Miha fighting the good fight in Ljubljana; my mother, who made me care about the arts, and my father, who made me think I could write books; also my sister, who was both the first person to listen to my musical recommendations and the first to stop; and most importantly Kaname, who's been just marvellous.

Ian Martin's writing about Japanese music has appeared in *The Japan Times*, *CNN Travel* and *The Guardian* among other places. Martin is based in Tokyo, where he also runs Call And Response Records.

CPSIA information can be obtained
at www.ICGtesting.com
Printed in the USA
LVOW12s1429250317
528463LV00001B/200/P